FROM THE BIBLE-TEACHING MINISTRY OF

CHARLES R. SWINDOLL

PRACTICAL
Christian Living
A Road Map to Spiritual Growth

40 DAYS TO A MORE MEANINGFUL LIFE

INSIGHT FOR LIVING

INSIGHT'S BIBLE APPLICATION SERIES

PRACTICAL CHRISTIAN LIVING
A Road Map to Spiritual Growth

From the Bible-Teaching Ministry of Charles R. Swindoll

Charles R. Swindoll has devoted his life to the clear, practical teaching and application of God's Word and His grace. A pastor at heart, Chuck has served as senior pastor to congregations in Texas, Massachusetts, and California. He currently pastors Stonebriar Community Church in Frisco, Texas, but Chuck's listening audience extends far beyond a local church body. As a leading program in Christian broadcasting, *Insight for Living* airs in major Christian radio markets around the world, reaching people groups in languages they can understand. Chuck's extensive writing ministry has also served the body of Christ worldwide and his leadership as president and now chancellor of Dallas Theological Seminary has helped prepare and equip a new generation for ministry. Chuck and Cynthia, his partner in life and ministry, have four grown children and ten grandchildren.

Based upon the original outlines, charts, and transcripts of Charles R. Swindoll's sermons, *Practical Christian Living: A Road Map to Spiritual Growth* was developed by writers in the Creative Ministries Department of Insight for Living as one of the volumes in our Insight's Bible Application Series:
John Adair, Th.M., Ph.D., Dallas Theological Seminary
Laura Singleton, Th.M., Dallas Theological Seminary
Michael J. Svigel, Th.M., Ph.D., Dallas Theological Seminary

Published By:
IFL Publishing House
A Division of Insight for Living
Post Office Box 251007
Plano, Texas 75025-1007

Editor in Chief: Cynthia Swindoll, President, Insight for Living
Executive Vice President: Wayne Stiles, Th.M., D.Min., Dallas Theological Seminary
Theological Editor: Brianna Barrier Engeler, M.A., Biblical Studies, Dallas Theological Seminary
Content Editor: Amy L. Snedaker, B.A., English, Rhodes College
Copy Editors: Jim Craft, M.A., English, Mississippi College
       Melanie Munnell, M.A., Humanities, The University of Texas at Dallas
Project Coordinator, Creative Ministries: Kim Gibbs, Trinity Valley Community College, 1991–1993
Project Coordinator, Communications: Karen Berard, B.A., Mass Communications,
       Texas State University-San Marcos
Proofreader: Paula McCoy, B.A., English, Texas A&M University-Commerce
Cover Designer: Margaret Gulliford, B.A., Graphic Design, Taylor University
Production Artist: Nancy Gustine, B.F.A., Advertising Art, University of North Texas
Cover Image: Copyright © 2008 Jupiterimages Corporation

ISBN: 978-1-57972-782-6
Printed in the United States of America

Table of Contents

A Letter from Chuck

Travelers dot the landscape of literature. Remember Christian, the everyman traveler in John Bunyan's *The Pilgrim's Progress*? He traversed the treacherous road from the City of Destruction to the Celestial City far beyond his imaginings, resisting temptations to leave the path along the way.

Christian knew where he was going, but he had to overcome tremendous obstacles along the way. And while it took him longer than he may have expected, he reached his destination. The Christian life is a journey much like his. It has a beginning and an end. Its path is littered with dangerous obstructions and precarious curves. And its destination provides lasting, eternal rewards.

Chances are you have experienced, as I have at times, the difficulty of losing your way along the path. Just like Christian, we have been tempted to stray, exchanging the fundamentals of our faith for more immediate fulfillments. This devotional, *Practical Christian Living*, reminds us that the goal isn't just reaching our destination but paying attention to how we get there as well. It calls us back to a life devoted to the Scriptures, to prayer, and most importantly, to Christ Himself. Remember, we can never outgrow the basics . . . we only build upon them!

My hope is that the devotional you hold in your hands will serve as a road map that will keep you traveling in the right direction—"fixing our eyes on Jesus, the author and perfecter of faith" (Hebrews 12:2). We are all on the same journey, a winding and perilous trek that will take those who follow Christ to the heights of heaven.

Only one question remains . . . do you remember the best way to get there?

Chuck Swindoll

Charles R. Swindoll

How to Use This Devotional

Accepting God's free gift of salvation and eternal life is the glorious first step in a long journey toward spiritual maturity. To that end, *Practical Christian Living: A Road Map to Spiritual Growth* begins with the initial moment of decision for Christ and describes in practical terms what the Christian life should look like beyond that life-changing commitment. Written in a convenient daily format, these devotions will help you focus each day on an aspect of the Christian life. God calls us to grow ever closer to Him as we follow Him along the path of life's twists and turns. It's an adventure worth taking!

Using the Devotional

Practical Christian Living: A Road Map to Spiritual Growth is designed with both individual and group study in mind. Each of the ten themed sections is divided into four days for easy use as a personal devotional over a forty-day period (or it may be modified for self-paced study). Groups will find the section divisions to be helpful, making it possible to use the devotional as a ten-week study.

If you choose to use this devotional in a group setting, please keep in mind that some of the devotions ask personal, probing questions, seeking to elicit answers that reveal an individual's true character and challenge the reader to change. Therefore, the answers to some of the questions in this devotional may be potentially embarrassing if they are shared in a group setting. Care, therefore, should be taken by the group leader to prepare the group for the sensitive nature of these studies, to forgo certain questions if they appear to be too personal, and to remain perceptive to the mood and dynamics of the group if questions or answers become uncomfortable.

Whether you use this devotional in groups or individually, we recommend the following method:

Prayer — Begin each day's study with prayer, asking God to teach you through His Word and to open your heart to the self-discovery afforded by the questions and text.

Scripture — Have your Bible handy. We recommend the New American Standard Bible or another literal translation, rather than a paraphrase. Each day you'll be prompted to read relevant sections of Scripture and to answer questions related to the topic. You will also want to look up Scripture passages noted in parentheses.

Questions — As you encounter the questions, approach them wisely and creatively. Not every question will be applicable to each person all the time. Use the questions as general guides in your thinking rather than rigid forms to complete. If there are things you just don't understand or that you want to explore further, be sure to jot down your thoughts or questions.

Our hope is that you will find this devotional a valuable part of your spiritual journey. May God richly bless you as you study His Word and seek to become more like Christ.

PRACTICAL
Christian Living
A Road Map to Spiritual Growth

How Can I Become a Christian?

1

God has made numerous promises throughout the Scriptures, but none is more significant than His offer of eternal salvation through His Son, Jesus. Motivated by His love for humankind, God desires to renew His relationship with us—a relationship that has been broken and marred by human sin and rebellion. So God chose to send His Son to earth. Jesus died on the cross for our sins, rising from the dead that we might live with Him for eternity. All that remains for each one of us is to accept His offer of salvation. Will you trust in Him?

The Love of God

Read John 3:16.

Every Christian's spiritual journey begins with God — He loves us and wants a renewed relationship with us. He loves us as His creation, confirming that love through His dealings with us. God's love is evident in the act of creation itself, granting life and existence to every human being, each of whom is made in His image (Genesis 1:26). But it also extends to all of God's acts in history. His love was behind the parting of the Red Sea (Exodus 14:26–31); His love for righteousness inspires His acceptance of the just and judgment of the wicked (Psalm 37:28); and of course, His love motivates His desire to renew our broken relationship with Him: "God *so loved* the world, that He gave . . ." (John 3:16, emphasis added). (You can read more about Jesus's sacrificial death and resurrection in the Bible. Try starting with the book of John.)

In the Old Testament, God's people had been punished and suffered the consequences of their sin against Him. Yet He promised to rebuild and renew them all the same. According to Jeremiah 31:3–4, why is God going to renew His people?

What will this renewal look like?

What attitude should all of God's people have in light of this promise?

Our God is a God of renewal, a God of rejuvenation, and a God of healing. He loves us; He's not out to get us. He isn't sitting and waiting for the day we trip up so that He can send us to hell. He has created each one of us with care, shaping and forming us before we were born and knowing us intimately (Psalm 139). His love ensures that He will provide a means of restoring our broken relationship so that we might spend eternity with Him.

Sometimes our tendency as fallen human beings is to focus on our own failures rather than on God's grace. We can allow ourselves to wallow in self-pity rather than to embrace His offer of mercy. We struggle with despising ourselves rather than accepting God's love for us.

Do you ever struggle with feelings of guilt over your sin and shame about who you are? Explain.

How do those feelings affect your decision-making? Do you find yourself making unwise decisions based on them?

How would your life be different if you lived in light of the truth that God deeply loves you?

Remember that God loves you and He wants a relationship with you. Embrace this truth and allow His love to illumine every aspect of your life.

> *Dear Father, I thank You for Your love. Sometimes, when I'm weighed down by guilt and fear, I struggle to believe that You love me. But I know that Your Word says You do. Help me, Lord, to accept Your love, to believe in it, and to live in light of it.*

Day 2

Our Separation from God

Read John 3:1–7.

After beginning with the recognition and acceptance of God's love for us, the spiritual journey continues with an acknowledgement that we are sinful and separated from God. Sin entered the world through Adam and Eve in the garden of Eden (Genesis 3). As a result, it has spread to all of humankind (Romans 5:12). Because we are sinful and God is holy, our relationship has been damaged. We have separated ourselves from Him; therefore, the bond between Creator and creation needs to be renewed.

In John 3, Jesus reminded Nicodemus of this need, though he did so using rather cryptic language: "Unless one is born again he cannot see the kingdom of God" (John 3:3). The need for rebirth in order to enter God's kingdom parallels the need for the renewal of our relationship with God. And the "born again" language offers a significant insight into this journey—just like in the physical realm, the process of spiritual birth does not occur of our own volition. We don't earn it. We don't clean ourselves up first. We don't even start by going to church. Covering our sins is accomplished by God, not by us. It is rooted in His work, not in ours. It is a result of His unlimited power, not our limited abilities.

Read Romans 3:10–12. Who is sinful, according to these verses?

What does Romans 3:23 reveal about our relationship with God?

According to Romans 3:24–26, who will justify (or save) those who have faith in Jesus?

Sin can be a tricky subject in today's world. Sometimes we overestimate our goodness or underestimate our responsibility for our failures. When we do, we may not see our need for Christ. We are tempted continually to deal with our sin on our own, rather than allowing God to care for us according to His plan.

How have you tried to deal with your sins in the past? Do you often find yourself trying to make amends for your moral failures on your own?

How does your approach to your sins impact your relationship with God?

Now is the perfect time to confess your sins to God and to ask Him to forgive you for your wayward actions and inactions. He promised that He will (1 John 1:9). You can count on it.

> *Dear heavenly Father, I know that I am a sinner in need of a Savior. I take full responsibility for my failures, knowing that only You can truly bridge the gap between us. May I see myself as I am, but always by the light of Your grace and mercy.*

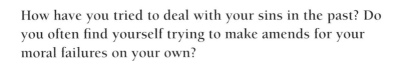

Day 3
Jesus: God's Provision

Read John 3:14–15.

A third element in our spiritual journey to God involves acknowledging Christ as God's only provision for sin. Through Christ's death on the cross, we are forgiven our disobedience. His resurrection ensures that we are spared the eternal punishment we deserve for our sin. Jesus's words in John 3 look forward to the cross by comparing it to the time in history when Moses lifted up the bronze serpent to heal the Israelites from the venomous bites of serpents that plagued the people as punishment for their rebellion (Numbers 21:4–9). As the people looked up at the serpent, the remnants of the poison left their bodies, healing the people from the effects of their sin.

The cross does the same for human sin. Through the cross, Jesus made the complete payment for sin. His death fully satisfied the demands of a holy God against sinful humanity. God told Moses to fashion a bronze serpent to heal the people from the poison of serpents. So, too, did God send His Son that humanity might be healed from the disease of sin that infects us all (2 Corinthians 5:21). As we embrace Christ's sacrificial death on our behalf, He heals us and passes on the gift of eternal life with God.

Read Hebrews 12:2. What does the writer of Hebrews want us to do?

How does this relate to Jesus's example of Moses and the bronze serpent in John 3:14?

According to Colossians 1:20–22, what is the result of Jesus's death on the cross?

Not only did Christ die on the cross for us, but He also rose from the grave three days later. This bodily resurrection won the victory over death, making it possible to spend eternity with God (1 Corinthians 15:17).

In this modern world, it can be difficult to allow someone else to do something for us. We've been taught to be independent people who can take care of ourselves without the intervention of anyone else. We have come to prefer it that way. However, the very notion of Jesus dying for us and rising again means we have to open ourselves up to help from another. We have to accept His gift. We had not asked for His gift. We may not even have expected His gift. But His gift has already been given.

Not only do we have to acknowledge our need for another when we accept Jesus's sacrificial death and resurrection, but we also have to swallow our pride. We have to acknowledge that we cannot deal with our sin on our own and that therefore we aren't as capable as we might like to think. This goes against the grain of much of what we hear these days. Popular wisdom says we can do whatever we put our minds to and that there is no reason why we shouldn't have whatever we desire in life. Jesus's death on the cross flies in the face of such a notion in that it forces us to admit our own shortcomings and place our trust in someone other than ourselves.

Do you have a difficult time giving up control? Do you prefer to do things on your own? Why?

How does this attitude impact your relationship with God?

As you seek to relinquish control of your life to God, accept Christ's sacrifice on your behalf. He opens the way to spend eternity with God.

Dear Father, thank You for sending Your Son to die for me. Thank You for Your offer of salvation through Him. Thank You not only for making a way to cover my sin, but also for sending me an example to follow the rest of my life.

Accepting Christ's Sacrifice

Read John 3:1–12.

After the first part of his conversation with Jesus, Nicodemus claimed confusion. The teacher of Israel had been told twice that he needed to be "born again," a concept that clearly wasn't immediately understandable to him (John 3:4). He asked, "How can these things be?" (3:9). Jesus noted that Nicodemus would not believe Him regarding heavenly matters until Nicodemus first believed Him regarding earthly matters (3:12). So while Nicodemus thought his confusion was primarily related to his lack of understanding (an effect Jesus acknowledged), Jesus went on to root it in Nicodemus's unbelief.

Embarking on our spiritual journey includes believing in and accepting Christ's sacrifice and resurrection. God has made the offer of salvation. The only question that remains is how we will respond to it.

Read John 3:9–16. How many times do you see the word *understand*? How many times do you see the word *believe*?

Understand: _____

Believe: _____

What do these numbers reveal about the emphasis of Jesus's teaching in this passage?

Read Acts 2:44; 4:4; 13:12; and 17:12—a sampling of verses describing the early Christians. What characteristic is held in common among them?

With that commonality in mind, what do these passages suggest is a vital element of beginning the spiritual journey with God?

God can and will save us from our sins, renew our relationship with Him, and provide us with eternal life in His presence through Jesus. We need only to trust Him. However, trust involves giving up control and opening ourselves to the will of another. It means that we must often give up our own desires when they are contrary to those of the relationship. For we human beings, sinners every one of us, this can be a difficult task. Too often we prefer our own way to God's.

Do you consider yourself a trusting person, or do you tend to guard yourself closely? Give an example.

Read Romans 10:9. Will you believe in Christ today and commit to follow Him? Write a prayer of commitment to the Lord below. If you've already trusted in Him for your salvation and future, use this space to write a prayer of thanks.

God's love for His creation spurred Him to send His Son as a payment and a covering for our sin. Because we are separated from God by that sin, Jesus provides hope of eternal life with God. We need only accept His sacrifice on our behalf to begin the journey. Will you follow Him?

Dear heavenly Father, thank You for drawing me to Yourself and saving me. Salvation is a gift from You. I believe and trust in Jesus alone for the forgiveness of my sins. Help me to live a life that is worthy of Your Son's sacrifice.

How Can I Begin the Christian Life?

2

Whether we're new to the Christian life or we've had a personal relationship with Jesus Christ for many years, it's easy to quickly lose our footing. We fall into sin, or we become distracted by temptation. We forget the joy and gratitude we felt when we first accepted God's free gift. We lose sight of heaven in our pursuit of the earth. To get back on track, we need to return to the basics of the Christian life — to understand and embrace what it takes to live God's way.

Day **1**

Growing Up, Not Growing Old

Read Colossians 2:6–7.

The Christian life is a life of growing up in Christ, not just growing old on earth. Note the verbs in Colossians 2:7: *rooted*, *built up*, *established*, and *instructed*. These words imply that the question for believers is not how long we have been Christians but how much growing and maturing we have done since we made a decision to trust Christ. Are we different now than we were then? We've been forgiven and justified (saved) by God's grace, but are we living lives seasoned with that grace?

The Bible often exhorts people to be mature in Christ. For example, read Hebrews 5:11–14. What image does the writer use to illustrate the difference between the mature and the immature?

Think about the phrase "by this time you ought" in Hebrews 5:12. What does this phrase imply about the progression of the Christian life?

According to verse 14, what is the result of maturity or growing up in Christ?

Growing up in Christ can be accomplished in a number of ways, but one of the keys is spending time in the Bible. Of course, this involves reading God's Word regularly, but our commitment doesn't end there. We also need to study it, to memorize it, and to meditate on it. Study involves taking notes, comparing different passages, and even reading commentaries or other books that might shed light on the biblical text. Memorization takes the knowledge of Scripture a step further, creating an opportunity for the believer to take God's Word wherever he or she goes. Meditation involves keeping it in mind at all times, thinking about the Scriptures in relation to our daily activities.

We should also make sure that we hear the Bible read aloud and taught, a practice that points us to regular and committed involvement with a local body of believers. Not only is it encouraging to share in the teaching of the truth with like-minded people, but the relationships we build with other Christians provide vital support as we seek to live out the teachings of Jesus in our lives.

In the chart below, check off each of the ways that you experience God's Word.

Reading	
Studying	
Memorizing	
Meditating	
Hearing	

Which of the above practices are you most successful at carrying out? Why do you think it's the easiest for you?

Which of the above practices are you least successful at carrying out? Why do you think it's the most difficult for you?

What will you do to develop greater faithfulness in each of these areas? Be specific.

Reading	
Studying	
Memorizing	
Meditating	
Hearing	

Look for every opportunity to grow up in Christ, and seek to enhance your growth through regular exposure to His Word.

Dear Father, truly Your Word is a light to my path.
It has faithfully guided me to Your Son. Help me
to embrace Your truth and live it so that I might
continue to grow and mature in You.

Embracing a Life of Gratitude

Read Colossians 2:7; 4:2.

In light of these passages, we can see that the Christian life is a life that overflows with gratitude. Anyone allowing this principle to direct his or her life will certainly stand out in this day of complaining, grousing, grumbling, and disputing. Paul's encouragement in Colossians appears in the present tense, meaning that our gratitude is not a one-time event. Rather, it continues over a period of time. It becomes a habit. It becomes part of who we are and the way we think.

However, developing an attitude of gratitude doesn't come from within ourselves. It is rooted in the grace of God, who welcomes His people into His kingdom, into a renewed relationship with Him. In this way, gratitude is a heartfelt response to what God has done for us. And in gratitude we affirm God's grace in our lives, live in light of it, and seek to practice it day by day.

Read Hebrews 12:28. According to this verse, why are we to show gratitude?

What is the result of our gratitude?

In Colossians 4:2, Paul encouraged believers to be devoted to prayer, doing so with an attitude of thanksgiving. Out of deep gratitude toward God, we spend time in prayer, praising Him for His greatness, His majesty, His character, and His plan. We give thanks for who He is and what He has done. God wants our prayer life to be woven throughout with a grateful spirit that's based in what He has done for us in Christ.

But gratitude can also shine through in our lives in any number of ways outside the quiet of our prayer times. How might our relationships change if we were motivated by gratitude for knowing this person or that one? How might they change if we were grateful for the position God has placed us in to minister to his or her needs? How would our offices or classrooms change if we came with a spirit of thanksgiving for the blessing of work each day? Gratitude, when it is lived out, changes things drastically—not only in our own attitudes, but in the attitudes of those around us.

Would you consider yourself to be a grateful person? Why, or why not?

Take some time to practice an attitude of gratitude right now. Think about what you are thankful for in life. Jot down your thoughts in the space below.

Offer a prayer to God in gratitude for what He has done for you through Christ, and then expand your gratitude to include people and events in your daily life.

> *Gracious Father, I am so grateful for the sacrifice of Your Son. His gift has provided purpose and direction for my once-scattered life. Please allow my gratitude for the salvation You have provided to spread to every area of my life.*

Resisting Legalists and False Teachers

Read Colossians 2:8.

When dealing with teachers who twist the truth or those who would encourage a life filled with legalistic boundaries over a life of rejoicing in the freedom Christ has given us, the reality of God's grace becomes even more important. Paul used the imagery of imprisonment or slavery in this verse as he warned believers against falling captive to skewed philosophy, deception, tradition for the sake of tradition, social and cultural expectations, and worldly pursuits. He stood against those who would have liked to enslave believers with these ideas. Paul was squaring off against legalists and false teachers. He was appealing for people's freedom. In that sense, the Christian life is a life of resisting those who would bring us into bondage.

Paul urged believers two thousand years ago to be on the lookout for these traps, but his call is still relevant today. Churches in every corner of the world consist of people who would prefer to count lists of rules and regulations as proof of the true Christian life. Believers should beware of such communities, just as Paul was in his day. God's people need not attempt such control over others. We know that God alone is in control, and we know that the Bible offers plenty of direction on its own—the direction God intends us to follow—without adding our own rules.

Read Colossians 2:16–22. Briefly summarize what was happening to the Colossian believers.

What practices were these false teachers and legalists advocating?

According to verse 19, the legalists and false teachers were not _____.
What does this say about their relationship to the church?

What did Paul instruct the believers to do?

As we watch out for those who seek to place us in legalistic bondage, to chain us to their own made-up spiritual rules, we need also to be careful about that which isolates us from other believers, the body of Christ. Those who place others in bondage seek to separate from the larger body. Achieving isolation, erecting boundaries, and acquiring control are the constant pursuits of the legalist. We who mean to resist such advances must be careful about listening to just one teacher or preacher. The body of Christ is made up of many parts. Many voices and many personalities exist for a reason — God teaches us through the variety present in the body.

Have you been in a legalistic church setting in the past or known someone who was? What was that church like?

What were some of the rules the members were expected to follow that were not based on God's Word or His grace?

When a person escapes the trap of legalism, how might his or her relationships change?

What might a church without legalists be like?

Resist those who would bring you into bondage; beware of the trap of isolation that legalists so often set.

> *Dear Father, when I first came to You and trusted You for my salvation, You set me free from the bonds of sin. Help me, Lord, to continue to claim that freedom. Help me to resist those who would cause me to serve their interests rather than Yours.*

Day 4

Focus on Christ

Read Colossians 2:9–10.

Our focus on Christ determines the degree to which we will live our lives in a grace-filled manner. Therefore, the Christian life is a life that remains fully focused on Christ. He is at the center. Our principles for living are based on Christ. Our worship centers on Christ. Our position is that we are complete in Christ. Our obedience is to Christ. The Christian life is one that seeks to honor Christ in its every facet. Christians are to be focused on pleasing Him rather than focused on pleasing everyone who happens to surround us.

The centrality of Christ echoes throughout Colossians 2. Paul noted that false teachers do not teach according to Christ (Colossians 2:8). Believers, on the other hand, have been made complete in Him (2:10). Paul also taught that Christ is head over all things (2:10), that the reality of the world to come is found in Him (2:17), and that Jesus provides the source from which His body, the church, grows (2:19). The degree to which we are growing, grateful, or gracious depends on the centrality of Christ in our lives.

Read Colossians 1:15–18. Why should Christ be the center of our lives? Using this passage, list at least four reasons.

1.

2.

3.

4.

Certainly, Christ is supposed to be at the center of the Christian life. But we all know that living our daily lives with Him at the center is easier said than done. When the concerns of life arise, the difficulties sometimes outweigh our faithfulness. And when that happens, Christ gets buried beneath the latest drain on our time—a late assignment at work, an argument with a spouse, or a frustrating ministry situation. In those times, we need to step back and refocus, placing Christ in His proper position.

Would you consider your life to be fully focused on Christ these days? Why, or why not?

List three issues you are currently struggling with in your life.

1.

2.

3.

Write "me" in the center of one of the circles below. Write "Christ" in the center of the other. Then, in each circle, write out thoughts or attitudes you have about each issue you listed above, depending on whose perspective is at the center of your life. (You should expect the thoughts or attitudes to change between circles, depending on the perspective.)

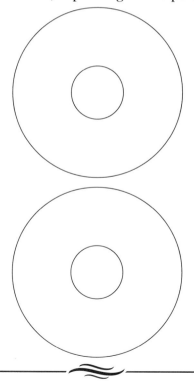

In the space below, reflect on the differences between how you would view these elements of life with you at the center of your life versus with Christ at the center of your life.

What steps can you take to keep Christ at the center of your life more consistently?

Living a life seasoned with God's grace is a direct result of being saved by His grace. Too often, people initially embrace the simple grace of salvation and then leave it behind for the complications of legalism, dissatisfaction, and self-focus. But if we place our focus on Jesus, we will find His grace is sufficient, not only for ourselves but for all His people.

Dear heavenly Father, Christ truly is the center of all things. In Him I live and move and have my being. In Him I can approach You with confidence. Help me keep Him at the center of my life.

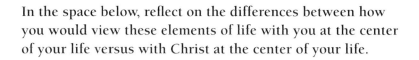

Ten Reasons to Give God Praise

3

Complaints and grumbling come so much more easily to us than praise and thanksgiving—this in spite of the fact that God has lavished us with His goodness and mercy. His ultimate act of love is His plan to save us from our sins. God has consistently acted on our behalf to bring us to Himself, and ultimately, to "seal" us—to make our salvation sure. In a world that seeks to undermine our confidence in the unseen, God assures those who believe in His Son that they will be forgiven and saved to spend eternal life with Him. For this, He deserves our praise.

Bring Glory to the Father

Read Ephesians 1:3–6.

The Christian life begins with the work of the triune God. Father, Son, and Holy Spirit—three persons in one—God sees the plight of humanity and acts to save us from the penalty we deserve for our sins. Then we have the opportunity to respond. In other words, the Father initiates salvation, so we glorify Him.

God the Father's involvement consists of three particular actions, each of which are reasons to praise Him. According to Ephesians 1:3–6: He "blessed us with every spiritual blessing" (Ephesians 1:3); He chose us "before the foundation of the world" (1:4); and He "predestined us to adoption as sons" (1:5). He has showered us with His favor, and because He has accepted us as His children, we share in the blessings reserved for His Son. He also chose us before anything was created. Before time began, before the earth existed, before we were created . . . God knew all that would be. And so, as a result of His love for us, He selected and adopted us as His children. While we were lost in our sin and rebellion, God reached out and brought us to Himself, making us His adopted children. God has taken all of these actions on our behalf, and so our response should be one of praise to Him, acknowledging Him as the loving and compassionate One.

Read Colossians 3:12; 1 Peter 2:9; and 2 John 1:1. What is the common factor in these descriptions of God's people, the church?

Since God's people have been chosen for salvation, what does that imply about God's role in the process?

Because we cannot earn our salvation and must therefore leave it in God's hands, how does His promise in John 10:27–28 affect your thinking about the security of our salvation?

We were adopted when we believed, we believed because we were chosen, and we were chosen in line with the spiritual blessings God sought to pour out upon us. Because God's action lies at the root of our salvation, we can trust that it is secure. If our salvation depended on us and our momentary impulses, we would have no firm basis on which to trust. God's work graciously provides assurance for us.

Take this opportunity to jot down a few areas or situations in your life in which you need to trust God.

Have you struggled with feeling assured of your salvation in the past? Why, or why not?

Will you commit to trusting Him for your salvation? How about for everything else?

As you recall God acting on your behalf in the process of salvation, give Him the glory that He deserves while taking confidence in the assurance He provides.

> *I glorify You, Father, for Your gracious work on my behalf. Your willingness to take me in as an adopted child can only be explained as an act of love and compassion. Help me, Lord, to glorify You as I should, as Your appreciative and eternally grateful child.*

Offer Worship to the Son

Read Ephesians 1:7–8.

While it is the Father who initiated His plan of salvation, it was the Son who carried it out. Jesus acted on the Father's behalf within our world. As such, we recognize that the Son saved us, so we worship Him. Ephesians 1 presents three reasons to praise Him that help to clarify the significance of the Son's saving work on the cross.

First, the Son redeemed us through the shedding of His blood on the cross (Ephesians 1:7). Christ came and died for us. His blood became the payment that satisfied the Father's righteous demands against our sin. Because of the cross, we have been set free. When Christ died and rose again, He removed the curse from us (Galatians 3:13) and won the victory over sin and death for us, releasing us from bondage. Second, in His act on the cross, Jesus offers us the forgiveness of our sins (Ephesians 1:7). He has removed the darkness of sin that separated us from God, clearing the way for us to walk in the light with Him. Finally, Christ provided these gifts because of the richness of His grace (1:7–8). There is more than enough grace to go around, a truth that should prompt us to turn toward Jesus in worship.

Write the dictionary definition of the word *redeemed*, or define it in your own words below.

Read 1 Peter 1:18–19. How were we redeemed?

In your own words, why do we need redemption?

According to Psalm 103:3–4, 12, how does God regard the sins of His people?

When we worship Christ, we ascribe worth to Him. We declare Him to be more worthy than anything else. Giving up His life for us on the cross was a completely selfless act on the part of Jesus. In the same way, to offer Him true worship, we must act out of a completely selfless motive. We recognize that we deserve nothing based on our own merit, that the salvation we possess comes as a gift from Him. Indeed, our very ability to offer Him worship from a purely selfless motive is also a gift from Him, a gift to be cherished.

Using your dictionary again, write the definition of the word _worship_.

On a personal level, why would you choose to worship Jesus? Give several specific reasons.

What obstacles get in your way when you seek to worship selflessly?

Take a few minutes now to worship Jesus personally.

We worship the Son of God, Jesus Christ, for His redeeming and forgiving work on the cross that has freed us from the bondage of our sin and given us freedom in Him.

> *Dear heavenly Father, thank You for Your Son and His work on behalf of all humanity. The redemption You offer through His death on the cross is dear to me, though not yet as much as it should be. Make my appreciation for His work more complete through the worship I offer You.*

Day 3

Give Honor to God

Read Ephesians 1:9–12.

Not only did God provide salvation through the Son, but God also implements His plan through Christ, so we honor the Son. Ephesians 1:9 offers one reason to give God praise, telling us that God has made known His plan. This has happened in the fullest sense through Christ, as the apostle John tells us (John 1:18). The plan itself involves "the summing up of all things in Christ" (Ephesians 1:10). In other words, because Jesus has made salvation available to everyone, believers from all over the world will be brought together in Him. As Paul taught elsewhere, the believers of the world are one in Christ, and "there is neither Jew nor Greek, there is neither slave nor free man, there is neither male nor female" (Galatians 3:28).

Second, salvation through Christ means not only that all believers have been made one in Him, but also that we will share in an eternal inheritance—a life with Him for eternity (Ephesians 1:11). Notice that the inheritance was instituted with God's plan and purpose. It is a done deal. It cannot be taken away from those who are in Christ. It will never diminish. It will never lose its value. It's ours through Jesus, so we honor Him for His irrevocable and eternal gift.

We are heirs to an eternal inheritance. Read the following passages and paraphrase each one in your own words.

Acts 20:32

Romans 8:16–17

Colossians 1:12

How do these promises encourage you about the security of your salvation?

Our response to God in light of His gifts to us is simple: honor Him. When we honor someone, we show him or her respect. Much of modern society, especially in Western culture, has lost a strong and clear sense of honor in our relationships with one another. In the name of honoring ourselves, we indulge ourselves by acting upon whatever desires we might be feeling at the time. When we honor someone else, we force ourselves to act based upon a standard outside of ourselves rather than upon our own impulses.

If honor means giving respect to another, what might it look like to honor another person?

Whom do you honor? Why?

What would it look like in your life for you to honor Christ?

In a world that has turned from honoring others to honoring self, make a point to give honor to God as He works out His plan in Christ.

Dear Father, sometimes it is difficult for me to honor You as I should. Please continue to bring to mind the eternal inheritance that awaits me and help me to have confidence in Your Son, Jesus, who has provided it.

Praise the Holy Spirit

Read Ephesians 1:13–14.

When it comes to our salvation, the Father initiated. The Son redeemed and implements. And finally, the Spirit sealed us—so we praise Him. When we heard and believed the message of the gospel, the Father sent the Holy Spirit to seal us in Him (Ephesians 1:13). God has brought us into His family, a gift that cannot be renounced. This "sealing," or making permanent, provides a guarantee of our future inheritance, namely, a life with Him for eternity (1:14). With the sending of the Spirit, not only does God promise something for the future, but His presence serves as a down payment on that promise.

Read 2 Timothy 2:19 and describe the seal believers have received.

Based on what we have learned in these last four days as we've studied this passage, how has our inheritance been ensured?

When we feel doubts about our eternal inheritance, where then should our focus be? (For help, see Hebrews 12:2–3.)

Note the presence of "praise" in Ephesians 1:14. God's work on our behalf should inspire praise. He has predestined us "to the praise of the glory of His grace" (Ephesians 1:6). He has provided an inheritance that inspires praise in those who hope in Him (1:12). And the Spirit's coming looks forward to a time in the future when God will redeem all of His creation, also a praiseworthy event (1:14). While it is tempting to focus on the daily ups and downs of life, it becomes clear that God deserves all our attention in praise, especially when we grasp the impact of His work on behalf of His creation.

Brainstorm several reasons for you to praise God.

Think back through the reasons to give God praise and offer Him thanks for His work.

1. He blessed us with every spiritual blessing
2. He has chosen us
3. He has predestined and adopted us
4. He has redeemed us
5. He has forgiven us
6. He lavished His grace on us
7. He made known the mystery of His will
8. He has provided an eternal inheritance
9. He has sealed us in Christ
10. He has guaranteed our inheritance

What a list! We can all have complete assurance of our salvation through Jesus Christ. When we believe that God has initiated this process, that His Son has carried out the plan, and that His Spirit is present in our lives, we can see the sovereignty of God in action and praise Him.

Dear heavenly Father, thank You for the sealing of the Holy Spirit. Thank You for the inheritance You have promised to all who are Yours. Please remind me to place my confidence in You, rather than in my own abilities, to bring about my salvation.

Handling the Scriptures Accurately

4

"You can prove anything you want from the Bible!" Have you ever heard someone say that? Probably. For the most part, it's true! If a person really wants to find biblical justification for some belief or action—and if he or she is willing to quote half-verses, rip passages out of context, and twist the meaning of words—then that person can "prove" just about anything from the Bible. We need to develop good habits and cultivate correct methods of handling the Word of God so that we can avoid engaging in or falling victim to spiritual abuse. As we develop good habits, we'll also become better students, interpreters, and appliers of Scripture.

Day 1

Guarding against "Scripture Twisters"

Read 2 Peter 3:14–18.

We've all known people who have twisted Scripture or taken it out of context, trying to make it say something that suits them. Sometimes people distort Scripture without realizing it, but others do it with intentional malice and deception. In either case, the results are often the same: we or other people are left with the impression that the Bible teaches something it does not. And if we embrace the faulty interpretation or application, we run the risk of harming our own spiritual health and negatively influencing the faith of others.

Unfortunately, Scripture twisters can be incredibly difficult to spot! Many appear sincere, personable, popular, and charismatic, and some even tout the titles of "Reverend" or "Ph.D." next to their names. In fact, some of them may be your own friends, family members, coworkers, teachers, or church members. But whoever they are—and regardless of their motives—Scripture twisters and Bible abusers need to be avoided. And, just as importantly, each of us needs to make sure we're not among them.

What two words does 2 Peter 3:16 use to describe those who distort the Scriptures?

Based on these words, describe the opposite kind of person, one who would be better equipped to handle Scripture accurately.

According to 2 Peter 3:17, what should believers do to avoid false teachings?

What does 2 Peter 3:18 say is the goal of reading and understanding Scripture accurately?

Jesus ran into Scripture twisters throughout His ministry (see Matthew 12:1–8; 15:1–6). And if Jesus encountered and had to correct these false teachers, what will prevent us from encountering them ourselves? More important, what will prevent us from *becoming* those who mishandle God's Word?

Have you ever had an encounter with a Scripture twister? If so, describe the circumstances.

What made you realize that this person was not handling Scripture accurately?

How would you know if you were handling the Bible inaccurately? What can you do to feel more confident in your understanding of Scripture?

Be on your guard against Scripture twisters and false teachers. If Christ had to face them, so will you.

Heavenly Father, I confess that, apart from a growing understanding of Your truth and ways, I am always in danger of misunderstanding or mishandling Scripture. Never let me forget what I am handling when I open the Bible: Your perfect Word. Teach me, Lord, to handle the Scriptures accurately, so I will neither be deceived nor deceive others.

Holy Bible: Handle with Care

Read Nehemiah 8:1–9.

The account of Ezra's reading of the Law—the Old Testament Scriptures—to the people of Israel paints a picture of how to handle the Scriptures accurately. From this passage we discover at least four basic truths.

First, accurately handling the Scriptures starts with reading them (Nehemiah 8:1–3). Like the Jews in Ezra's day, we can benefit when we simply read Scripture, allowing God's Word to sink deeply into our hearts. Note that Ezra read from early morning to midday, paying close attention to the words (8:3).

Second, accurately handling the Scriptures includes having respect for them (8:3–5). The Bible is not a collection of people's opinions. Just as Ezra and the Scriptures were located above the people as a symbol, we must place ourselves under Scripture's authority, never standing in judgment over it. And just as the people stood up when the Law was read, we need to purposefully respect God's Word.

Third, accurately handling the Scriptures means explaining the truth for all to understand (Nehemiah 8:7–8). Note that the Levites explained the Law to the people, moving big truths from the top shelf to the bottom so they would be accessible to all. The meaning of Scripture doesn't always jump out of the text. We can gain insight as we listen to godly preachers and teachers, read books, use study aids, and become involved in a church devoted to studying and applying God's Word.

Fourth, accurately handling the Scriptures results in obedience to the Scriptures (8:3, 6, 9). The Israelites paid attention to God's Word, responding with agreement, worshiping the Lord in reverence, and repenting of their past failures. Likewise, when we probe Scripture to seek understanding of what God expects of us, we must obediently heed His Word.

Read Ephesians 4:11–12. List the five kinds of people God gave to the church for the purpose of building up the body of Christ.

Besides the apostles and prophets who were inspired by God to write the Scriptures so many centuries ago, who are the God-gifted evangelists, teachers, and pastors who teach you the Word today—either in person or through their writings? Name two people and explain how they have helped you better understand and apply God's Word.

We can glean much from our time spent in both personal and group study of God's Word by applying a fourfold Bible-study method of observation (what does it say?), interpretation (what does it mean?), correlation (how does it fit together?), and application (how does it work in my life?). To make these steps easier, serious students of Scripture should work together, gaining wisdom from older Christians, insight from scholars past and present, and inspiration from those who lived out God's Word faithfully through the ages.

If somebody were to say, "I don't need anything or anyone to understand the Bible," how would you respond?

According to Ephesians 4:12–16, what is the role of the Christian community in your growth in knowledge and truth? What is the responsibility of each individual member— regardless of whether or not he or she is in leadership?

When it comes to reading and studying God's Word, you shouldn't go it alone! God has given you a whole history and community of helpers to guide you along the way to understanding and living His Word.

Father, I want to know You better by knowing Your Word. But I confess that left to my own resources I am just as susceptible to pride, self-deception, and error as anybody else. I ask that You teach me through my personal Bible reading, through gifted pastors and teachers, and through Your church.

Understanding Christ as the
Center of Scripture

Read Luke 24:25–32.

What's the Bible all about? The answers to that question may be as numerous as the people you ask. Some think it's all about God's miraculous work in history. Others think its main purpose is to communicate great stories that teach spiritual and practical wisdom. Many think the point of the Bible is to preserve God's lists of dos and don'ts along with examples of what happens when you obey or disobey.

However, Jesus gave the best answer when He told the two disciples on the road to Emmaus that "all the Scriptures" pointed to Him (Luke 24:27). On another occasion, He said, "All things which are written about Me in the Law of Moses and the Prophets and the Psalms must be fulfilled" (24:44). Then Jesus "opened their minds to understand the Scriptures" (24:45).

Jesus is at the heart of Scripture. In Him the message, theme, purposes, and principles of the Bible come together.

According to the following passages, how do the Scriptures relate to Jesus?

Romans 1:1–4

1 Corinthians 15:1–5

2 Timothy 3:14–15

When you read the Bible, do you keep Christ at the center? Do you let the text drive you to Christ? Do you find its fulfillment in Him? In our reading of Scripture, we must never forget to ask such questions as:

- What does this passage teach about Christ's person or work?

- What problem does this text raise, and how is Christ the solution?

- How does this passage illustrate something about the perfect character of Christ? How can I follow His example?

How might an awareness of the role of the Bible in pointing forward or backward to Christ affect how you read it?

As you read various sections of the Old Testament, ask yourself how they reveal aspects of Christ's character or work. It might help to first make a list of words that describe Christ (wisdom, justice, grace, mercy, sacrifice, and so forth). Then, explore how the Old Testament texts highlight or contrast with these characteristics. This method of study can make the Old Testament come alive for you in ways it never has before. Choose one of the following passages, and try this method in the space below: Genesis 22:1–4; Deuteronomy 10:18; Psalm 23; or Proverbs 2:6–7.

Because Jesus is the center of the Bible, no portion of Scripture, even of the Old Testament, is properly read, understood, or applied until it leads us to Christ.

Heavenly Father, thank You for the all-encompassing knowledge of Your Son, Jesus Christ. Help me to keep Your Son, the Living Word who became flesh, at the center of Your written Word, the Bible. As I open Your precious Scriptures, let my heart be led to its true Heart, Jesus Christ.

Moving from Knowledge to Action

Read James 1:22–25.

A spiritual famine ravages most of the Christian world. It is not a shortage of churches, mission agencies, or evangelistic ministries. It's not a shortage of Bibles, Christian literature, or gospel tracts in hundreds of languages. No, the spiritual famine that plagues the world is a shortage of people living by the Word of God.

This world is filled with hearers of the Word . . . but it starves for doers of the Word. The Bible was not given to fill our heads with knowledge but to fill our hearts with faith, hope, and love. Of course, we can't have the right heart without the right knowledge, but we *can* have the right knowledge without the right heart. Although Paul prayed that believers would have "a spirit of wisdom and of revelation in the knowledge of [Christ]" (Ephesians 1:17), he also warned that "knowledge makes arrogant, but love edifies" (1 Corinthians 8:1).

What are the purposes of God's Word according to the
following passages? Write just one or two words that
summarize your conclusions.

Psalm 119:105

James 1:25

2 Timothy 3:16–17

Five simple standards will help us handle Scripture
accurately—standards summarized in *what*, *who*, *why*, *where*,
and *when*.

First, never forget *what* you're handling. It's God's
Book—God's voice. This will keep you sensitive to what your
Creator has to say to you.

Second, always remember *who* has the authority. The Lord
Himself speaks authoritatively to you through the Word. This
will keep you humble as you submit to Him.

Third, keep in mind *why* you're studying. Remembering that you're trying to discover and apply God's meaning will keep you accurate.

Fourth, think about *where* you are. Coming to the Bible with your questions, needs, and problems will keep you attentive to God's answers, provisions, and solutions.

Fifth, focus on *when* your study ends. Studying Scripture doesn't end when you run out of time or when you've learned something new. It ends when it has made a difference in your life. Reminding yourself of this truth will keep you practical.

Which of the five principles do you feel you've neglected most in the study of God's Word?

Which do you think you've kept most consistently?

Write the main *what*, *who*, *why*, *where*, and *when* principles in your Bible and review them each time you study the Scriptures. By handling the Scriptures accurately, you will be better able to spot and avoid Scripture twisters, be more attentive to keeping Christ central, and be more likely to passionately pursue what God calls you to do.

> *Father, I want to be a doer of the Word, not merely a hearer. Make me sensitive to what You want to say to me. Make me humble before Your authority. Keep me accurate in my understanding. Make me attentive to my need for living the truth You reveal. And keep me practical as I drink deeply from Your living waters.*

Prayer: Calling Out

5

Most Christians say they believe in prayer with all their hearts, but many admit that they neglect prayer for weeks on end. To this day the apostle James's first-century statement haunts us: "You do not have because you do not ask" (James 4:2). Many believers would openly confess that they fail here more than in any other area of the Christian life. How about you? Aside from a quick prayer before meals, can you honestly say that you are a person of prayer, that you truly are one who has consistently cultivated a life of intimate communication with God? If your answer is yes, that's wonderful! But you are the exception rather than the rule.

Day 1
The Priority of Prayer

Read 1 Timothy 2:1–3.

We hear a lot about getting our priorities right . . . putting first things first . . . keeping the main thing the main thing. Having begun a relationship with God and having made Him the center of our attention and worship, what do we do next? Paul's letter to his protégé, Timothy, turns our attention to what Paul regarded to be of vital significance. Before anything else, he began, "I urge, then, first of all, that requests, prayers, intercession and thanksgiving be made for everyone" (1 Timothy 2:1 NIV).

Though God's Word constantly encourages us to pray, today's Christians often treat prayer as an afterthought. Instead of being the conscious first step in making life decisions, prayer becomes a forgotten footnote. Rather than a first response to a crisis, prayer becomes the last resort. Though our lives would benefit incalculably from making prayer a top priority, it often gets chewed up and spit out by the daily grind.

Have you seen evidence that prayer is being put on the back burner these days? Why do you think this is so?

In the following passages, prayer is made a priority. Jot down the key words that indicate the importance of prayer.

Acts 2:42 *life together a common meal prayer*

Acts 6:2–4

1 Thessalonians 5:17 *be cheerful thank God no matter what happens*

Clearly, prayer was a top priority for Paul and the first Christians. And it should be for us. Before you set off on a job search, entreat God. Before you fret about your finances, petition the Father. Before you partake of His gifts, thank the Giver. From the profound to the petty, from the massive to the mundane . . . immerse your life with prayer.

Describe your current practice of prayer. When do you pray? For how long? How do you do it? With whom?

Are you satisfied with your current practice of prayer?

Where would you place prayer in your list of priorities? If prayer is not a major priority for you, why not?

As you think about your day-to-day life, what specific changes would help you make communication with God a greater priority? Will you make them?

Consistent prayer is a biblical priority for the Christian life. Is it a priority in your life?

Dear Father, thank You for the gift of prayer. I am sorry for not receiving that gift with open arms, for failing to make it a priority, and for sometimes treating it more as a duty than a privilege. Work in me, Lord, that I may treat prayer as a joy rather than a burden. Help me, Lord, to experience a greater intimacy with You through a lifestyle of prayer.

Day **2**

The Purpose of Prayer

Read 1 Thessalonians 5:16–18.

In conjunction with rejoicing and thanksgiving (1 Thessalonians 5:16–17), the apostle Paul regarded prayer as "God's will for you in Christ Jesus" (5:18). But why? Why is prayer so important for the Christian life? What exactly is it?

Simply put, prayer is communicating with God. Prayer is co-laboring with God to participate in the accomplishment of His will in our lives and in the lives of others. It involves trust, surrender, devotion, and commitment. When we fail to understand what prayer is, we can fall into a misapplication of its principles. Prayer is not bargaining, bartering, or playing "Let's Make a Deal." Prayer is not a painful marathon of monotonous misery, nor an opportunity to show off one's spirituality. It's not a magical formula to get what you want from God, nor is it a means of manipulating the Almighty into giving us what we want. The purpose of prayer is not to bend God's will to our own but to align our will with His.

Read Matthew 6:5–8. Note three observations about prayer that you see in Jesus's words.

Read Matthew 6:9–13. How does this model prayer differ from your typical prayers? List at least three contrasts.

Because of a lack of understanding, most of us have probably misused prayer in the past. On the one hand, we may have treated God like a vending machine or stubborn employer rather than a loving heavenly Father who responds to us in ways that glorify Him and demonstrate His love for us. We may have chosen to handle things on our own and neglected prayer altogether . . . or we may have gone to the other extreme, replacing our own timely action with prayer and shirking our responsibilities. Clearly, there are a lot of perils involved when we misunderstand the purpose and principles of prayer.

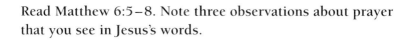

Consider the following potential perils, reflecting on how you may have stumbled over each of them.

Irresponsibility. Prayer is not meant to *replace* human action or responsibility. The two work together in a mysterious way. How have you used prayer as an excuse for passivity or laziness?

Misperception. If we picture God as an angry ogre, our prayers will most likely be timid and few. If we see Him as a pampering parent, they can be self-centered. How has your perception of God's character sometimes misguided your prayers?

Oversimplification. Sometimes we can turn prayer into magic words that seek to get us what we want when and how we want it. How have you treated prayer like a formula rather than an intimate conversation with our Lord and God?

Prayer is communicating with God—on His terms, not ours. Avoiding common perils of prayer will help you enjoy an uncommon life of prayer.

> *Dear heavenly Father, reveal to me the ways I have misunderstood and mistreated prayer. Where I have been irresponsible, prompt me to act. Where I have misperceived You, help me to know You better. And where I have oversimplified prayer, let me experience the excitement of a dynamic communion with You.*

Day **3**
The Promises of Prayer

Read 1 John 5:14–15.

Prayer can take numerous forms—speaking or singing . . . sighing or shouting. We can pray silently in our minds, in whispered fragments, or even in desperate screams. Regardless of *how* we pray, we can be assured of at least four clear promises attached to prayer.

First, God promises He will hear and answer, regardless of the timing (1 John 5:14–15). We don't have to stand in a queue waiting for our turn. We don't have to wonder if He's listening. We can have confidence that our loving, powerful God is the One who hears our prayers (Psalm 65:2).

Second, God promises His presence, regardless of the outcome (2 Corinthians 12:7–10). When we ask God to act in our lives, He may choose to answer immediately, or He may delay or deny the answer we request in order to bring about a greater good we could not have foreseen in our limited knowledge.

Third, God promises to carry our weights and burdens, regardless of how heavy or extensive they are (Philippians 4:6; 1 Peter 5:6–7). Our worries, concerns, fears, and struggles may feel like too much to bear. But when we go to Him in prayer, He will carry the full weight of those burdens for us.

Fourth, God promises inner peace and relief, regardless of the chaos and complication (Philippians 4:7). When we pray, we exercise faith. And as that faith strengthens, God gives us an incredible sense of peace and security in Him.

Read Matthew 7:8–11. Does God give us everything we request? What do you feel are the limits based on Matthew 7:11?

In 2 Corinthians 12:7–10, how did God provide for Paul in spite of the fact that He didn't answer his prayer in the way Paul asked and hoped?

What does "good" mean in the context of Romans 8:28 and James 1:17? How might "good" in our minds differ from God's perfect knowledge of what is "good" for us?

Because He is all-knowing, all-powerful, and all-good, God can be trusted to answer our prayers in the right ways and at the right times. He can even be trusted to delay or deny requests that He knows would harm us. Yet in this dynamic fellowship of prayer with the Almighty, He promises to hear us, to be with us, to bear our burdens, and to grant us peace.

For each of the following passages, summarize in a few words the "good" we can receive from God through prayer.

Ephesians 1:18

Philippians 1:9

2 Thessalonians 3:1

James 1:5

James 5:14–16

Which of these benefits of prayer is most encouraging to you today?

    You can trust our loving and powerful God to answer your prayers for your good, not harm—even when painful times tempt us to doubt this truth. Are you willing to trust Him today?

> *Dear Father, I come to You today with so many needs, hurts, and struggles. You know the details of my circumstances better than anybody. You know them even better than I do. I ask that You work things together for Your glory and for my good—whatever that may be. Because I trust that You are all-good and all-powerful, I ask that Your will be done.*

The Peace of Prayer

Read Philippians 4:6–7.

The pressures of our times have caught many of us in the web of one of the most menacing sins: worry. Worry is not an emotion; it's a choice. Worrisome people choose fretting over entrusting an issue to God's care. Worry is wrestling with the bully of anxiety on your own rather than letting the Father fight your battles for you. The choice to worry creates unrest, prolongs uneasiness and, if left unchallenged, churns our waves of anxiety into a storm of destructive emotions.

Prayer is the God-ordained alternative to worry. As we lift our joys and burdens to God through regular, faithful, intimate communication with Him, He will replace our worry with peace, our burdens with blessings, our anxious mutterings with songs of praise.

According to Philippians 4:6, what are the alternative responses to persistent worry?

Which of these alternative responses is your usual response to persistent worry? If none apply, how do you usually respond?

According to Philippians 4:7, what does God promise to those who choose prayer instead of worry?

The peace that comes from God and the protection of our hearts and minds through prayer will allow us to have joy even in the midst of troubling circumstances. Yet our primary goal in calling out to God through a life of prayer is not to make our daily existence easier or more enjoyable. The goal can be summed up in three words: intimacy with God.

Select one of the following practical applications below to help you implement a more consistent lifestyle of prayer in your relationship with God:

❏ Commit to pray every day for the specific needs of a specific person. Write his or her name here:

_____

❏ Keep a "worry notebook" and note the things that occupy your thoughts and emotions during the day. Each morning, turn this "worry notebook" into your prayer guide.

❏ Ask a close friend or family member what things are worrying him or her, then commit to pray for his or her worries this week.

Remember that prayer is the antidote to worry . . . and the means of lasting peace in the Christian life.

Dear heavenly Father, I confess that I am deeply concerned about many things. I accept now that these are beyond my ability to resolve, and I release them into Your hands. Please help me to be more aware of the needs of others, to commit my concerns to prayer as a common practice, and to give You the thanks, glory, and praise You deserve.

Shedding Light on Our Dark Side

When we accepted the forgiveness Christ bought for us on the cross, His blood washed away the penalty for our sins . . . but not our ability to sin. Yet with the new life in Christ given to us as a free gift and with the Holy Spirit working to bear fruit in our lives, we have something we did not have before our salvation—the ability to resist temptation and refuse to sin. Understanding how sin affects us and what can be done when we sin will help us get a handle on living the Christian life. Unless and until we shed light on our dark side, we will be confused and unable to walk in victory over sin.

The Battle Raging within Us

Read Galatians 5:16–23, 25.

A battle rages in the lives of believers, a conflict within each of us between our sin nature—our human propensity to fall short of God's standard—and the new righteous nature we possess by God's saving grace. Paul described these two forces as the desire of the flesh and the desire of the Spirit (Galatians 5:17). This internal conflict of dueling desires manifests itself as either the "deeds of the flesh" or the "fruit of the Spirit" (5:19–23). In every believer, these forces square off; and in every skirmish with temptation, we have a choice to make—will we ally ourselves with the Spirit's campaign for spiritual freedom or join the doomed insurgency of the flesh?

As long as we are living in our mortal bodies in this corrupt world, we will be consumed by this internal conflict. On the one hand, there is evil, wickedness, and wrong—the "flesh." On the other hand, there is righteousness, good, and truth—"the Spirit." We serve one or the other as we travel this road of spiritual growth. And until our journey ends in God's heavenly city, the battle rages on.

According to Galatians 5:16 and 19, what is the source of our wicked deeds?

According to Galatians 5:22, what is the source of our righteous deeds?

What is the result of the opposition between our flesh and God's Spirit (see Galatians 5:17)?

Becoming a Christian is not synonymous with becoming a model of perfection. We "live by the Spirit" (the Holy Spirit dwells within us), but we are also encouraged to "walk by the Spirit" in our daily lives (Galatians 5:25). Because we are still sinners by nature, we can become sinners in practice — that is, we *can* and *do* lose the battle against the flesh. For Christians, living above the practice of sin is not automatic. Rather, it's the result of winning daily battles against the flesh by the power of the Holy Spirit living in us. Prior to salvation we lacked the supernatural ability to battle against sin. Because of the Holy Spirit, we have something we did not have before our salvation — the ability to resist temptation and refuse to sin.

Which of the "deeds of the flesh" mentioned by Paul in Galatians 5:19–21 afflicts you the most?

According to Galatians 5:16, what must you do to avoid carrying out the desire of the flesh? (We'll discuss the practical *how* of this later on.)

Galatians 5:24 says that believers have crucified the flesh. This means you have been freed from its absolute, tyrannical power over you—though we are responsible to act in accordance with this truth. How does the defeat of the power of the flesh by the death of Christ inspire you to square off against the passions and desires of your flesh with confidence?

Never forget that the greatest battle a Christian must fight is the internal battle with the desires of the flesh . . . a battle that can be won only by the power of the Holy Spirit.

Father, thank You for saving me by Your grace and setting me free from the bondage of sin. I acknowledge that apart from Your Spirit working in me, my flesh will yield only weeds of wickedness. Please produce in me abundant fruit through the Holy Spirit living in me.

Day 7

Fighting against Our Fleshly Desires

Read Romans 7:14 – 21.

We've all lived these verses in Romans 7 more days than we can remember — more days than we'd like to admit. We start the day combing through Scripture, bathing ourselves in prayer, and dressing in the garments of righteousness, ready and willing to take on all the challenges ahead of us with faith, hope, and love.

Then we hit breakfast. Something spills, and if we don't grit our teeth in anger, we blurt out some angry exclamation that squashes the spiritual fruit of patience. We snap at our children, throwing out love, kindness, and self-control. Arguments and grumbling kick in, and soon our lives are devoid of peace and joy. On the drive to work, billboard images catch our eyes and we dwell on them far too long — there goes goodness and faithfulness. By noon our optimistic promises to live like a saint crumble into the paralyzing reality of the frailty of the flesh.

In the following verses, what terms did Paul use to describe the sinful nature that causes our good intentions to fail in everyday practice?

Romans 7:17, 20

Romans 7:21

Romans 7:23

Read Matthew 26:37–41. Contrast Christ's will (26:39) and the will of the disciples (26:40). What caused the disciples' inability to do what they knew to be right?

According to Matthew 26:41, what was Jesus's solution?

Day after day, month after month, year after year, the lingering power of our fallen flesh ambushes our good intentions and takes us hostage to sin. When it happens we feel like crying out with Paul in frustration, "Wretched man that I am! Who will set me free from the body of this death?" (Romans 7:24).

Is there a specific habit or pattern of sin that comes to mind when you reflect on Paul's description of the "willing inability" in Romans 7:14–21? Describe your struggle.

How does it make you feel that the apostle Paul himself struggled with this conflict between the willingness to do good and the failure to follow through?

In the midst of this agonizing conflict, Paul was able to write, "Thanks be to God through Jesus Christ our Lord!" (Romans 7:25). What do you think gave him the ability to write this? (See Romans 8:1–2.)

You may feel down and defeated by repeated failures in your war against the flesh. Take heart! All believers fight the same war . . . and we can rejoice that there is truly no condemnation for those who are saved by Christ.

Father God, I stumble and fall in so many ways, but I want to thank You for freeing me from condemnation because of the cleansing power of Your Son. I know that though my spirit is willing, my flesh is weak. I pray that Your Spirit will strengthen me as I take steps to live more and more in victory over this abiding nature of sin.

Day 3
The Gift of Grace

Read 1 John 1:5–10.

Once in a while you'll come across Christians who expect perfection—not only from themselves but from you too. They have been deceived into thinking that because they are born again and have the Spirit of God living within them, they should no longer sin. Or they may believe that as Christians, they have been given the power and ability to live in continual holiness without ever stumbling.

Don't be deceived! The reality is that "we all stumble in many ways" (James 3:2). Only a perfect man does not stumble—and there has only been one perfect Man who lived a life without sin—Jesus Christ (Hebrews 4:15). John said that if we claim to be without sin, we are lying (1 John 1:8). All of us are victims of our "sin nature"—that propensity to do what we know is wrong. But all believers also have a means of cleansing our lives from acts of sin. We will never be perfect, but that does not excuse us from seeking to become more and more like Christ by the power of the Holy Spirit.

t the "if . . . then" statements in
), and complete the following statements in
·ds:

1:6 — "If we say that we have fellowship with Him and yet walk in the darkness . . ."

1:7 — "If we walk in the Light . . ."

1:8 — "If we say that we have no sin . . ."

1:9 — "If we confess our sins . . ."

1:10 — "If we say that we have not sinned . . ."

As adopted children of God, we will always be part of God's family. Nothing—not even our sins—can separate us from His love (Romans 8:38–39). However, just like children of human parents, our relationship with our heavenly Father can be affected by our disobedience and rebellion against Him. Though He will never disown us as children, He will discipline us as a father disciplines those He loves (Hebrews 12:7).

Is your relationship with your heavenly Father a little rocky? Are you avoiding time with Him because of unconfessed sins? Do you feel yourself drifting farther and farther from His loving gaze? It's never too late to confess your sins and return to the light of His grace.

What specific sins have you left unconfessed today?

Take this opportunity now to bring these to your heavenly Father and let Him wash you clean, restoring your fellowship with Him.

Even as Christians we are still sinners, and our sins affect our daily fellowship—not our eternal relationship—with God. But if we confess our sins to God, He will make us pure and clean before Him. Out of His grace, we are forgiven every time we ask.

Father, I admit that I am a sinner saved by Your grace. I often take advantage of Your grace and sin against You. I want to confess my sins to You now. Please forgive my sins and cleanse my heart.

Day 4

The Victory over Sin

Read Romans 6:1–10.

Do you feel worn out by spinning your wheels in the muck of sin? Are you fatigued from fighting the battle against sin? Do you sometimes feel like throwing up your hands and surrendering to the constant barrage of attacks from your sinful nature, temptations from Satan, or seduction from the world?

Don't give up! The battle against the insurgency of sin in our lives will never let up until our mortal bodies are transformed into glorified bodies, when we will gain the ultimate victory promised by our Almighty Commander-in-Chief (1 Corinthians 15:51–57). Until that time, however, we are called to consider ourselves dead to sin but alive in Jesus Christ (Romans 6:11).

Romans 6:11–13 gives several direct orders that believers are to follow to prevent sin from reigning over them. Can you find at least three?

Read Romans 12:1–2 and 1 Corinthians 10:13. With regard to resisting temptation and sin, note at least two of God's provisions or promises and at least two of your responsibilities.

Divine Promises/Provisions:

Human Responsibilities:

Until the glorious day when we experience final victory over sin at the coming of Christ, we can employ specific strategies to help us recover from the sudden assaults of temptation and the setbacks of sin. Here are some very practical ways to "walk in the Spirit." Remember, your own strength cannot accomplish these things, but these steps will allow the Holy Spirit to work out His will through you.

Read each of the following four practical ways to overcome sin. Then consider how well you are implementing them in your own life, with 1 being poorly and 5 being successfully.

1. **Keep short accounts with God. Don't let a lot of time elapse between your sins and your confession.**

Poorly   Successfully

1   2   3   4   5

2. Stay in close touch with God's people. Don't be isolated from fellowship with other believers.

Poorly   Successfully

1   2   3   4   5

3. Refuse to rationalize your wrongs. Don't make excuses, don't play cover-up, and don't hide your sin from yourself and others.

Poorly   Successfully

1   2   3   4   5

4. Learn to say "No" by practicing it every day. Don't let yourself indulge "just a little," because little sins inevitably grow into big sins.

Poorly   Successfully

1   2   3   4   5

Though we will have constant conflict with our sin nature in this life, the Holy Spirit stands ready to help us win victories over sin. With confidence in His power, prepare for battle!

Heavenly Father, help me to consider myself dead to sin but alive to You through Christ. By Your Spirit, help me to resist temptation and overcome the weakness of my flesh. By Your grace, give me victory.

Is the Spirit's Filling That Big a Deal?

A person speaking in unintelligible gibberish . . . a woman dancing and lifting her hands in worship . . . a man falling to the ground, overcome by an unseen force or feeling. What exactly does it mean to be "indwelt by the Spirit" or "filled with the Spirit"? Fortunately, God's Word can guide us as we seek to answer these questions. We know that the Spirit indwells every believer when he or she accepts God's free gift of salvation through Jesus Christ. We also know that God commands us to be filled with the Spirit and to yield to His control—Scripture often illustrates the effects that the Holy Spirit has on believers' lives. And as we begin to study what traditionally has been a confusing and divisive issue among Christians, may we be careful to treat others with love and grace.

The Indwelling of the Spirit

Read 1 Corinthians 6:19.

B efore we can understand the filling of the Spirit, we must first comprehend His presence in our lives. Our salvation occurs as a result of the triune God working in perfect unity for our salvation. To think of God as a Trinity—in the unity of the one God there are three persons—is to understand that the Father, the Son, and the Holy Spirit are all equal in power but distinct in roles. God the Father draws us to Himself, and the work of Jesus Christ has provided salvation for all who will believe. When a person chooses to believe, he or she is immediately indwelt with the Holy Spirit, who resides or exists within our hearts, or inner beings. Everyone who accepts Christ as Savior receives the Spirit, who guides, prompts, and transforms us according to God's will.

As believers, we cannot receive Christ without also entering into relationship with the Father and the Holy Spirit. Therefore, even when believers aren't living in accordance with the Spirit, He is still with us. In 1 Corinthians, Paul wrote to the church at Corinth, a notoriously corrupt city where even the Christians were sloppy with sin. But in spite of their disobedience, they, too, were permanently indwelt by the Holy Spirit. Their behavior was a sign of their refusal to submit to the Spirit and allow Him control in their lives. If you are a Christian, the third person of the Trinity is with you, no matter what. While your commitment to the relationship may waiver, His never does.

Read Romans 8:9. Is it possible to be a Christian and not have the Holy Spirit? No -

The church in Corinth was known for its sinful behavior. When Paul admonished its members in 1 Corinthians 6:19–20, how certain was he that they were indwelt by the Holy Spirit? Is the indwelling of the Holy Spirit conditional, based on behavior? Why, or why not?

According to Ephesians 1:13–14, how does one know for sure that he or she is indwelt by the Holy Spirit?
once we believed
we were signed, sealed
by the 3 in one

It's easy to compare ourselves to other believers and wonder if we truly have the Holy Spirit within us. Do we have as much of the Spirit as they do? When our Christian lives are typified less by fancy "supernatural" manifestations than by gradual spiritual growth, we may doubt that we're indwelt with the same Spirit as others. Rest assured, no extraordinary outward manifestation of the Spirit is necessary in order to be a faithful follower of Christ.

Since you trusted Christ for your salvation, have you ever doubted whether you have the Holy Spirit living in your heart? Why, or why not?

Do you ever struggle with the idea that your sins or faults prevent the Spirit's indwelling? Why, or why not?

In your own words, explain how you can know for sure that the Holy Spirit is in you.

If you have accepted Christ as your Savior, the Holy Spirit is within you. No extra work, no extra sign, no extra step is needed to get the Spirit or to prove His presence.

Dear heavenly Father, I thank You for giving me Your Spirit when I trusted Christ, and I thank You for giving me a way to come near to You every moment by consciously submitting to the Spirit's leading. I pray that You would lead me, guide me, and use me today.

The Filling of the Spirit

Read Ephesians 5:17–19.

In the Christian life, our access to God comes through salvation. We're reconciled to the Father and adopted into His family through Christ's work on the cross. Upon salvation, we receive the Holy Spirit—not a part, or some, but *all* of Him. The Holy Spirit guides us, empowers us, and transforms us.

Therefore, if a Christian isn't growing in his or her spiritual life, is struggling with persistent sin, or is wrestling with incapacitating doubt, the problem isn't a lack of the Holy Spirit. What's missing is a volitional act of submitting to the control of the Spirit. The secret to spiritual maturity isn't getting more of the Holy Spirit; it's yielding more—giving the Holy Spirit control, a process Paul described as being "filled with the Spirit" in Ephesians 5:18. And Paul called all believers to be filled with the Spirit. God desires that we would yield control of our lives to His will for us. In this way, the fruit of the Spirit—love, joy, peace, and so on—will become the defining characteristics of our lives, rather than our inclinations toward various kinds of sin (Galatians 5:22–24).

Read Galatians 5:16. Observe the verbs in this verse. What action is present tense, and what is ongoing into the future?

In your own words, what does this verse mean? Think about specific attitudes, actions, or choices.

Submitting to the Holy Spirit isn't a one-time event. Yielding to His control in our lives requires a constant act of the will. Dedicating ourselves to God's will and purposes can become as regular as breathing when submitting to Him becomes a higher priority in our lives. And as we experience the filling of the Holy Spirit more and more often, we'll begin to notice more quickly when we're slipping away from His path for our lives.

Submitting to or being filled by the Spirit begins with confessing the sin that hinders our relationship with God and asking Him to help us yield to His will for our lives. In your spiritual life, would you characterize yourself as submitted to and filled with the Spirit most of the time, some of the time, or rarely? Why?

What areas of your life do you find easiest to yield control to the Holy Spirit? What areas tend to be the hardest to give up?

How do you know when you've slipped away from God's path? Are there certain events, emotions, or people that make remaining in the Spirit more difficult? Please explain.

How can you prepare for these situations?

Being filled with the Spirit requires an ongoing decision to yield control to the Holy Spirit and to seek God's will over our own.

Lord, I place myself and my situation into Your hands. I give You my life. Come, take control. Please guide me, transform me, and use me for Your will and Your glory. More than anything, I want Your will to be done in my life.

Day 3
The Fruit of the Spirit

Read Galatians 5:22–23.

Believers will experience results when they are filled with or live according to the Spirit. These results could be as simple as possessing an increased measure of self-control at the buffet line or as profound as experiencing joy in the midst of a terrible tragedy (Galatians 5:22–23). Like a healthy tree produces fruit, when we're filled with the Spirit, certain behaviors will be obvious.

What about believers who seem to have more of the Spirit than others? Some Christians emphasize physical manifestations of the Spirit (such as speaking in tongues, boisterous worship, or being "slain in the Spirit"), even using them as a test for spirituality or maturity. Others find themselves to be uncomfortable with those experiences, questioning if they can be supported by Scripture. Regardless of one's position, we must stay close to the teaching of Scripture, interpreting it carefully and accurately in order to avoid the temptation to create non-biblical tests for spirituality.

Christians may differ on some of the specifics regarding what "filling with the Spirit" looks like, but remember that Jesus loves and uses people in ways we may not agree with all the time. Therefore, we should be cautious and gracious toward one another.

Read 1 Corinthians 12:13. How many times does the word "all" occur? How many times does "some" appear? According to this verse, is it possible that some members of the body of Christ missed out on the *indwelling* of the Spirit?

Read Ephesians 5:18–21, and then outline the behaviors that will result when we are filled with the Spirit.

Galatians 5:22–23 lists some of the characteristics that develop in us under the Spirit's influence (the "fruit" of the Spirit). What traits are included?

Just as God designed each of us as a unique creation, so our experiences in the Christian life are also unique. The Holy Spirit works in and through our individual personalities to accomplish

God's will as we yield to Him. We must be careful to avoid creating non-biblical formulas for "proper" spirituality or using our different experiences to "rank" God's children.

Have you ever wondered about someone else's spirituality, or your own, based on the presence or absence of unusual manifestations (see examples on page 101) attributed to the Holy Spirit? Explain.

According to what you've learned thus far in the lesson, how can you tell if you are "filled with the Spirit"?

The Bible lists some of the results we'll see in our lives when we're filled with the Spirit. So stick closely to the Scriptures and avoid creating tests that we or others have to pass to prove the presence of the Holy Spirit.

> *Dear Father, I pray that You would open my eyes to the fruit of the Holy Spirit in my life. And please help me to conquer the temptation to judge myself or others based on the different ways the Spirit expresses His presence within and through us.*

Day 4

The Doctrinal Debate

Read Ephesians 5:19–21.

The beliefs and practices centered on the Holy Spirit have diversified much in the last century. With the Spirit often considered more mysterious than the Father or the Son, the uncertainty around Him has invited an assortment of perspectives. The resulting variety naturally leads to debates among otherwise like-minded Christians. Nevertheless, believers are called to embrace our commonality. Ephesians 5:21 calls us to bear with our differences in love because of our mutual allegiance to Christ.

Debate among believers is often healthy. Each of us should be constantly seeking to follow Christ and to grow in our understanding of God's Word. This pursuit requires careful biblical interpretation, which is best accomplished as we work together. Unfortunately, we sometimes become dogmatic, more concerned about proving our conclusions to be the right ones than about being "constantly nourished on the words of the faith and of the sound doctrine" (1 Timothy 4:6).

We must remember that within the boundaries of the essential truths of the Christian faith, the common ground we share is far greater than the areas in which we disagree. We are children of the same God, saved by the same Messiah, and indwelt by the same Spirit. The vast majority of our beliefs, our history, our values, and our future hopes we have in common. In light of all we share, we must extend grace and love toward our sisters and brothers in Christ.

Read John 13:34–35. What are we commanded to do in this verse? How will our obedience affect others?

According to Ephesians 4:2–3, what should be our attitude when we disagree with other Christians?

Read each of the following three passages. Then describe the specific actions we are encouraged to take.

1 Corinthians 1:10

Colossians 3:13–14

1 Peter 3:8–9

What is the overarching goal mentioned in these verses?

Remember, as Christians we have much in common, but we're not required to agree on every point. However, even in the midst of healthy doctrinal discussions with the purpose of accurate biblical interpretation, we must treat one another with love and grace.

If someone were to tell you that you don't have the Holy Spirit because you aren't speaking in tongues (or something similar), what would your response be, based on the Scripture covered in this lesson? What should your attitude be?

All believers receive the indwelling Holy Spirit at salvation. And while we might disagree about the meaning or the results of the Spirit's filling, we must always hold to the high standard of love as the context of our discussions.

> *Lord, please forgive me for all of the times I haven't treated people according to Your commands. Help me to tame my tongue, to show others the grace You've shown me, and to love them with patience and kindness.*

Jesus: He Is Lord

8

When we study the life of Jesus, we often consider the mystery of His incarnation, His miraculous birth from a virgin, His jaw-dropping miracles, the cruelty of His crucifixion, and the hope of His resurrection. His position as Lord over all is one truth that sometimes gets overlooked. Because He is Head over all the church and has first place in everything, it stands to reason that nothing falls outside the scope of His rule — including, of course, every aspect of our lives. When we understand His lordship over everything, we see our role as Christians much more clearly. He has called us to surrender our lives completely to Him.

Submitting to Christ's Authority

Read Colossians 1:13–19.

As we consider Jesus, one of the most significant facets of His person is His lordship—that He is Lord over all creation (Colossians 1:16). He carries with Him the authority over everything and everyone, a position given to Him by the Father. Because of that, our response should be one of obedience, which means surrendering our own desires in favor of His. Surrender is a vital step in becoming the men and women God created us to be. An attitude of surrender compels us to purposefully place every aspect of our lives under His authority and lordship. Surrender involves both releasing the wrong and embracing the right. It's a lifelong process to be sure, and we all embark upon it once we have trusted Christ for our salvation.

God wants us to loosen our grip on both the external and the internal facets of our lives. Externally, He asks His people to surrender our relationships and our work to Him. Surrender should characterize every relationship we have . . . with mom and dad, son and daughter, brother and sister, employer and employee, and friend and neighbor. Also, our work, or our calling, should be pursued in the knowledge that God has placed us in our role or position — yes, within the church and outside of it as well — for His purpose and plan (see Ephesians 4:11). Recognition of His lordship produces an attitude of surrender that permeates every task we undertake.

What reasons does Colossians 1:15–18 reveal as to why we should surrender to Christ's authority in our lives?

Read Ephesians 4:1–3 and Colossians 3:17. Acting "in the name of the Lord Jesus" means acting on His behalf, as if He were performing the action Himself. How might a surrendered relationship reflect a submission to Christ's authority?

How might a surrendered calling or work life reflect Christ?

Surrendering to Christ's ideal in our relationships and in our work can sometimes seem a monumental task. We'll often need to swallow our pride in moments of distress or conflict, take a courageous step for the good of all involved, or accept a leadership role when it isn't always comfortable. Any of these actions might be easy to do once or twice, but when they occur day in and day out, they become impossible for us to practice regularly on our own. However, if we rely on God and count on His grace working in our lives, we can begin to surrender more and more aspects of our relationships and our work lives to Him, trusting Him for the results.

Place a check mark next to the words below that describe the difficulties you most often experience in your heart as you relate to others.

Impatience	_____	Judgment	_____
Anger	_____	Unforgiveness	_____
Envy	_____	Pride	_____

Choosing one of the above, describe how this struggle is expressed in your life.

How can you become a better representative of Christ in those moments? What part does surrender to Christ's authority play in your plan?

Remember that Christ calls us to surrender every area of our life to His control—including our relationships.

Heavenly Father, as I strive to follow in the footsteps of Your Son, please continue to give me insight into the relationships and calling You have placed in my life. Allow me to be a faithful representative for You in all that I say and do.

Day **2**

Surrender and Service

Read Ephesians 4:14–16.

God desires for us to surrender every element of our lives to Him, including our circumstances and our bodies. When we first come to Christ, we come like little children—malleable, trusting, and eager to serve. However, those childlike qualities can also lead us into trouble, making us susceptible to being tossed by the waves and carried by the winds into false teaching and compromised living (Ephesians 4:14). That's the way of a child—up and down; happy and joyful one minute and wallowing in a flood of tears the next. So often our feelings, actions, or beliefs are based on shifting circumstances rather than strong convictions. We open ourselves up to paths that aren't pleasing to God, paths that are harmful to ourselves and to others.

In some cases, being directed by our circumstances will also place our bodies at risk of dishonoring God. When the body functions in line with the Head (that is, Christ), the Head will build the body up in love (4:16). Now, in Ephesians 4, Paul was speaking of the church body, but this truth can also be applied to our physical bodies. We each have appetites, habits, and temptations that influence our physical behavior. Are we truly serving Christ in our bodies as well as in our minds and our hearts?

It's much easier to make verbal claims or commitments of devotion to Christ in public than it is to follow through in private. But God calls us to follow Him, and He will make that possible by His grace. Ultimately, we must rely on Him for our success in placing both our circumstances and our bodies under His authority.

Read Colossians 3:5–11 and list the behaviors Paul called Christians to "put aside."

Now read Colossians 3:12–13 and list the behaviors Paul called Christians to "put on."

According to Colossians 3:17, what should motivate our words and actions?

God calls us to surrender our circumstances and our bodies, but the reality remains: this task can be one of the most difficult for believers. Simply put, circumstances are hard to bear. Our bodies often try our patience. Living the Christian life is not easy. Christ calls us ever closer, nearer and nearer to Him. Thankfully, Christ has sent us a helper, the Holy Spirit, the One who will give us strength as we let go of the control we grasp so tightly.

Surrender involves both letting go of the wrong and embracing the right. Look back at the lists you made of behaviors to "put aside" and "put on." Do you find it easier to give up a sin or to take on a godly behavior? Why?

Write out 2 Corinthians 12:9 (or another verse that speaks directly to the struggles you've listed above). Commit this verse to memory and recall it as temptations arise.

While the path is difficult, commit to surrendering your circumstances and your body to Christ's ideals for you.

> *Dear heavenly Father, I know that I sometimes allow circumstances or temptations to get in the way of serving You fully. Direct my steps, Lord, as I seek to overcome my weakness by depending on Your strength and grace.*

Taking Every Thought Captive

Read Ephesians 4:17–29.

God does not want us simply to acknowledge His lordship over the external elements of our lives. He also calls us to acknowledge Him as Lord over the internal elements, those areas of our lives less open to the scrutiny of others, such as our minds and our emotions. Paul exhorted the believers in Ephesians 4:17 not to live as everyone else, in "the futility of their mind[s]." A futile mind is darkened in its understanding, excluded from and ignorant of the godly life. It develops out of a hardened heart, leaving one callous, given over to lusts for both material and physical pleasures. However, when we submit our minds to Christ's authority and power, we will possess a heart open to God's leading, an attitude focused on the well-being of others, and a life lived in peaceful communion with God's people.

In the same way, when we surrender our emotions, it dramatically changes the way in which we live our lives. Emotions are not bad; in fact, they are a God-given part of us. But when our emotions lead the way, our behavior is unpredictable. Unstable or dominant emotions can lead us to lie when we feel cornered, push us to pridefully stand our ground when someone offends our sensibilities, or prevent us from letting go of resentment. However, when we yield our emotions to Christ, we act against our momentary impulses to lie, to cheat, or to hold a grudge.

Read each of the following Proverbs and summarize the truth they teach.

Proverbs 14:29

Proverbs 16:32

Proverbs 19:11

Proverbs 21:23

Proverbs 26:21

According to these verses, what are the results of controlled or surrendered emotions?

Too often we find ourselves rationalizing that our poor choices are the results of our emotions. While this might be true, it doesn't alleviate our responsibility for our actions, regardless of whatever feelings might be running through our veins at a particular moment. But poor choices could also indicate that we have not yet surrendered our minds to Christ. When we invite Christ in to reign as Lord of our minds and of our emotions, His plans and desires for our lives become primary and ours become secondary.

Describe a situation in which you allowed your emotions to direct your choices. What happened? What was the result?

If you could go back and handle this situation differently, what would you do? Why?

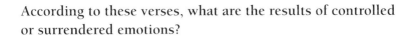

Read 2 Corinthians 10:5 and Philippians 4:8. How can we train our minds and emotions to be more like Christ's?

Choose one specific action from those listed in the verses to practice today. Which will it be?

Commit your mind and your emotions to the service of Christ, striving to bring honor and glory to Him through every thought and feeling.

Dear Father, You are Lord over all thoughts and emotions. You know the proper response in every situation. Help me, O God, to bring the internal areas of my life in line with Your values.

Day 4
Giving Up Your Will

Read Ephesians 4:30–32.

When it comes to the internal aspects of our lives, God also calls each one of us to surrender his or her "will" to God. The *will* puts into action the course that the mind or the emotions have determined. And ultimately, it is someone's will that sets him or her against God's will. Paul's list of offending actions in Ephesians 4:31 applies to each of us in some way: bitterness, wrath, anger, clamor, slander, and malice. The human will desperately needs to be reformed, a problem only God can solve. If a person allows his or her will to be conformed to Christ's, then that person's life can be emptied of the actions Paul condemned and filled with kindness, gentleness, and forgiveness.

Read Ephesians 2:1–5. What was our state before accepting Christ as our Savior and Lord?

What does that say about each individual's ability (or will) to be good on his or her own?

According to Philippians 2:13, who works out the good in us?

Allowing Christ to be Lord of our lives will end up costing us a great deal. He will ultimately require sweeping changes in our lives. We will begin to replace anger with gentleness, wrath with peace, and slander with self-control. We will learn to undertake every action in love, thinking of others before ourselves. But while Christ sets a very high standard for us, we do not embark on the journey alone. He has sent the Holy Spirit to accompany and transform us, helping us as we take each step toward Christlike living.

When you make life decisions, do you sense a struggle between your will and your desire to be like Christ? Explain.

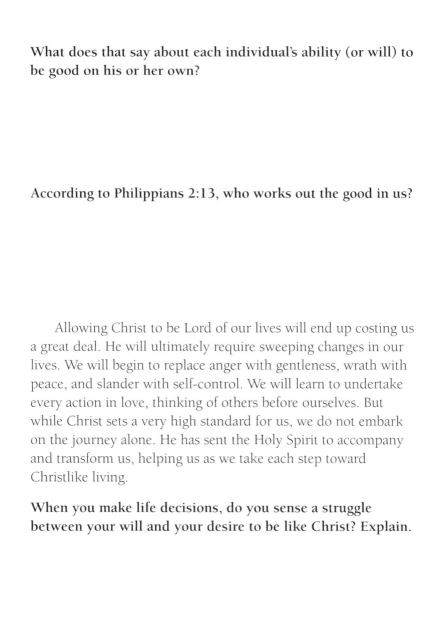

When you make a poor decision, what kinds of ideas, feelings, or thoughts tend to be at the root of it?

In what ways can you begin to submit your will to Jesus? Make a list of at least five specific actions you can take.

Surrender might have negative connotations in many circumstances, but we should understand its significance in light of Christ's call to follow Him. In both the external and internal areas of our lives, God calls His people to acknowledge the lordship of Christ.

Dear heavenly Father, help me to overcome the sinful desires of my will. I acknowledge my weakness before You, knowing that only Your strength and grace can renew all of me, both externally and internally. Renew my will, Father, and make it more like Christ's.

Discovering Your Part in Reaching the Lost

9

E ver tried to drink water from a fire hydrant? You probably wouldn't have much success. Fire hydrants release too much water for any one person to drink at one time. Too often our attitude toward spreading the gospel is the same; it's just *too much*. We feel there is too much to do—too many people to reach. However, we should be encouraged that sharing the truth about who Jesus is and what He has done for us can happen one person at a time. Jesus has given each one of us a significant part in reaching others with His message of forgiveness and grace (Matthew 28:19–20).

Are You Available?

Read Acts 8:25–28.

Many believers struggle with the task Jesus gave to His followers right before He ascended into heaven—to tell others the truth about who He is and what He has done for us (Matthew 28:19–20; Acts 1:8). As we seek to obey, our tendency is to focus on ourselves—especially on our fears or expectations regarding what might happen. God has called us to step outside of our comfort zones and to see the world from someone else's perspective. We need to make ourselves available for the opportunities that arise. Our availability begins with a sensitivity to God's leading in our lives. Like Philip, we must be willing to go where God leads (Acts 8:27). Jesus constantly made Himself available to others in His ministry. He was also aware of the needs of those around Him. Likewise, we should be attentive to the needs of people around us—physical, emotional, and spiritual. Will we follow His example?

In Acts 8:26–27, what command did Philip receive? What action did he take?

What does Philip's response suggest about his availability before God?

Read John 5:1–9. What needs did Jesus meet in this man's life? What might Jesus have sacrificed in order to be available to help him?

We can never predict how God will choose to use us in the mighty task of telling others about Him. Making ourselves available to others might require something as major as a move to another city or something as minor as an increased awareness of those around us in the lunchroom at the office. We need to seek God's leading in every situation. Even if it means changing plans at the last minute, will we be available for His purposes? Can we overcome our fears in order to share the truth about Jesus with someone? Do we regularly notice and attempt to meet the needs of those around us?

If you had the opportunity to tell someone about Jesus right now, would you be willing to do it? Why, or why not?

How might meeting the needs of another person be an avenue toward sharing Jesus with him or her? Give an example or two.

Think of a person you know who doesn't have a personal relationship with Jesus. What could you do to be more available to him or her? What needs could you meet in that person's life?

If you have the opportunity, how will you begin to share the truth about Jesus with that person?

Be sensitive to God's leading, make yourself available, and seek to meet the needs of others in order to share the gospel with those who do not yet know Christ.

Lord in heaven, I know that I can become self-centered, caught up in my own concerns and interests. But You have called me to be available to others. Help me, Lord, to be attentive to the physical or emotional needs and spiritual condition of those around me.

Day 2

Taking the Initiative

Read Acts 8:29 – 30.

Fear is one of the most common excuses we give when we don't share the gospel. Fear paralyzes us, rendering our legs immovable and our speech unintelligible. Our fear of looking foolish so often prevents our action on Christ's behalf. Philip, having received the command of the Holy Spirit to approach a stranger, obeyed and spoke up (Acts 8:30). He took the initiative, placing his desire to follow God's leading above his fear of what might happen or of what the other person might think.

Initiative plays a significant role in the lives of believers seeking to follow the commands and example of Christ. God teaches us that we have been created to do good works (Ephesians 2:10). Of course, to fulfill His plan for our lives, we will have to act, taking the initiative to pursue goodness and truth in certain situations. The Bible is filled with people who have done just that. Overcoming their fears, men such as Moses, Jeremiah, and Paul spoke the truth in the face of immeasurable opposition. But in spite of the difficulties they faced, the initiative that drove their actions was both honoring to God and significant in rallying God's people to do His work.

Read the following verses and describe God's perspective on fear in His people.

Psalm 56:11

Jeremiah 42:11

Acts 27:24

What do these verses suggest about the place of fear in the life of the believer?

Think about 2 Timothy 1:7 in the context of sharing Christ with others. Rather than with fear, how should we approach these opportunities?

We can take the initiative to share the truth about Jesus in a couple of ways. First, our actions can be the beginning of meaningful conversations. Taking food to a sick neighbor, giving up a seat on the train, or offering to spend a Saturday helping an older relative can eventually lead to significant discussions about the willingness of Christ to give of Himself. In the same way, a well-placed question in general conversation or an intriguing topic during a shared meal can turn any dialogue toward the gospel. Whatever the approach, if we take the initiative, sharing Christ can become an integral part of any relationship we have or acquaintance we make.

What are some questions you tend to ask people when making general conversation?

Take one of those questions and describe how it could provide an opportunity to talk about spiritual issues. Look for opportunities to use that question this week.

Regardless of our good intentions, remember that no one will hear the gospel unless we take the initiative to share the truth with others.

> *Dear heavenly Father, You have given believers*
> *access to Your power, love, and self-control. I know*
> *I have no reason to fear when I am in Your service.*
> *Transform me, Father, giving me the initiative*
> *possessed by your Son as I seek to share the truth*
> *with others.*

Day 3
Listen before You Speak

Read Acts 8:31–34.

When sharing the gospel with others, we often have to overcome a certain stigma associated with being "religious." Those outside the church possess certain ideas about what Christians are like and what we believe. Their assumptions are not always correct, though they are often deep-seated and confidently held. Many people have had negative experiences with judgmental Christians, legalistic churches, and the like. So we must carefully approach others with tact, recognizing their hurt rather than rushing to defend.

Notice that after Philip initially engaged the man in Acts 8, he allowed the Ethiopian to ask his question. Philip didn't simply hear the first phrase, decide he knew what the man was talking about, and offer a canned answer. He waited. He listened. He responded with tact. And what was the result? The eunuch invited Philip to ride in his chariot, they read the Scriptures together, and the Ethiopian asked Philip for his interpretation of a passage from Isaiah. Now, would this have happened had Philip jumped in immediately without listening to the man? Probably not. People tend to be more open to listening when they feel that they're being listened to. And Philip, by employing a little tact, was able to share the gospel with this man.

Paraphrase each of the following passages in your own words.

James 1:19

Colossians 4:5–6

1 Peter 3:15

How does good listening and the use of tact play a role in our interactions with those who don't yet know Christ?

Tact not only involves a patient and listening posture toward others, it also extends to the way we speak. Hemming and hawing, shifting eyes, and a generally uncomfortable demeanor certainly give off an extremely negative impression, contradicting our declaration of confidence in the gospel we claim to believe.

Too often when we're sharing the gospel, we present ourselves in a way that says we are uncertain about these truths or that we're only sharing because we feel as if we should. Instead, possessing a firm inner belief, we should be able to speak boldly, with strong eye contact, a winsome attitude, and a compassionate spirit. In this way, we can know our personal testimony about the power of Christ's crucifixion and resurrection will come from a place of genuine concern and care for another person.

Are you a good listener or do you tend to dominate conversations? Plot your position on the graph below.

Good
listener

Dominate
conversations

What elements do you think are essential to tactful and courteous conversation?

Which of these elements do you consistently practice?

Which ones do you need to work on?

Practice courtesy and tact by listening to others well, sharing your faith with confidence, and doing it all with a winsome attitude.

> *Dear Father, Your Son's example and Your Spirit's power provide me the direction I seek and the ability to accomplish Your will. I know that others need what You have graciously given me. Help me to share Your truth with confidence and a concern for others.*

Day 4
Taking Action

Read Acts 8:35–40.

Sharing the gospel effectively requires us to be available, to take the initiative, and to exercise tact in our conversations with those who do not yet know Jesus. However, the truth will only be heard if we are decisive. Ultimately, we must decide to forgo any feelings of discomfort, fear, and inadequacy to tell someone about Jesus Christ—to speak clearly and confidently about Him.

Having heard the Ethiopian's question, Philip opened his mouth and spoke about the Old Testament Scriptures, explaining how they point forward to Jesus Christ (Acts 8:35). Where the Ethiopian eunuch stumbled in the darkness, Philip shone the light of Christ. Where the Ethiopian was lost in his ignorance, Philip brought knowledge of the Son. Philip answered the man's question with confidence, boldness, and kindness. And the Ethiopian believed.

What command does Jesus give us in Matthew 28:19?

How do you think decisiveness plays into fulfilling that command?

So many opportunities slip through our fingers—imagine who we might meet on a plane, who might work out next to us at the gym, or who might sit next to us in the lunchroom. Why are these people where they are, in such close proximity to us? Because God has placed them there. The tragedy is that some of us might see these people every day and let a year pass without one mention of Christ. A commitment to decisive action will ensure that we speak the truth every chance we get.

Have you shared the truth about Jesus with anyone in the last six months?

If so, describe what happened.

If not, what has discouraged or prevented you from engaging others with the gospel?

Draw on what you've learned in this lesson and write out a plan for sharing the gospel the next time you have the opportunity. What will you say, do, or think?

While availability, initiative, and tact are significant, decisiveness is the key to whether or not you actually share the gospel. Choose now to look for and act on any opportunity God sends your way.

> *Dear heavenly Father, help me with my decisiveness.
> I can remember many opportunities I had to share
> but did not. Fill this hole with Your strength and
> power, that I might rely on You as future opportuni-
> ties arise.*

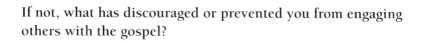

The Church: Who Needs It?

10

As we mature in our Christian faith, one of the most significant realizations we will reach is a healthy understanding of and appreciation for the church. Most of us go through great difficulty as we come to this conclusion. During our spiritual "growing-up years," the church usually suffers the brunt of our criticism and the bulk of our complaints. We go through periods of ignoring and resenting the church, and then we travel to the other extreme of virtually worshiping the church. Therefore, we need to come to terms with the biblical role of the church and its God-given place in our lives.

Practicing Faith within the Church

Read Hebrews 10:24–25.

Before He was crucified, the Son of God declared to the apostle Peter, "I will build My church" (Matthew 16:18). From this simple statement, we see that the church belongs to Christ. He is the Head of the church. Therefore, the major focus of His work is centered on His people, all believers from throughout the ages who make up His church. In fact, our membership in Christ's universal church begins at the moment we trust Christ for our salvation. We are then part of the body of Christ, spiritually united with Him and with one another (1 Corinthians 12:12–13).

God has also called each one of us to regularly participate in the life and ministry of a local church for the purpose of mutual encouragement and spiritual growth (Hebrews 10:24–25). We need to bring that faith out of our minds and hearts and into the physical world where we dwell—to be a part of His local body, united with believers not just in belief but in the practice of our faith. Sharing our lives with like-minded believers allows us to learn from others, to serve, to be challenged to change, and to experience joy and suffering in community.

Read Ephesians 2:19–22. How did Paul describe those who know Christ? What is our relationship to one another, according to verse 21?

Compare this passage to 1 Corinthians 12:14–18. Why is it necessary for each person to be connected to other believers through the local church?

Sadly, many people choose to live out their Christian faith outside of the context of the local church. Frequently, this is due to a failure on the church's part to be what God intended—a group of people committed to Christ and therefore willing to sacrificially love and serve each other. While this troubling state of affairs is all too common (and worse, accepted) in our fallen world, avoiding regular participation in the physical community of Christ's followers will leave a significant hole in the identity of the individual believer. It also hinders our ability to live out Jesus's teachings during our time on earth, giving us fewer opportunities to grow spiritually and become more like Christ.

Do you consider yourself to be a vital member of a local church? Why, or why not?

Are there any reasons that are preventing you from becoming part of a local body of believers? What are they?

What would it take to get you more involved in a Christian community? Be specific.

Commit to taking the next step in becoming a vital part of a local church, participating actively in its life and ministry.

Lord in heaven, the church belongs to You. I know that, as a believer, I'm part of the church. Help me to live out my true identity as one of Your children, coming together with Your family as a regular and meaningful part of my life.

Pursuing Healthy Relationships

Read Romans 12:4–13.

M any times Christians will talk about their faith as a "relationship" with God. While that's true, when we become believers, we receive more than a renewed relationship with God. We also enter into a whole new set of relationships with His people. We are accepted into the family of God. In fact, God refers to believers as His children on numerous occasions (see John 1:12). With the commitment of "family" supporting us, we are encouraged to pursue healthy, God-honoring relationships in the context of the local church.

In Romans 12, Paul gives an idea of what such a community or family might look like. Each person is accountable to everyone else—we are part of one another (Romans 12:4). No one can live as an island in the church. What one says and does affects others, and vice versa. So believers are meant to encourage the good in each other (12:9). We serve, protect, honor, pray for, take care of, and love one another (12:10–13). And those who are mature in the faith model truth for those who are new believers.

Read the following "one another" passages describing the actions Christians are to perform. Then give a possible real-life example of each.

Ephesians 4:32

Philippians 2:3

1 Thessalonians 5:11

If we embraced the perspective of these verses by exhibiting a willingness to serve others in every part of our lives, how would that change the way the world perceives the church?

Of course, just like in families, the relationships we have in the church don't always work as they should. We constantly need to be reminded by the spiritual leadership in our church of how we are to live. We need the example of those who are older and wiser, who have learned the hard lessons of self-denial and of how to love their neighbors as themselves. The church is the place to practice the ideal of healthy relationships. And because we are all practicing, we need to prepare ourselves to make mistakes, to seek forgiveness, and to offer it. All healthy relationships need a hearty dose of grace, and what better place to find that than among God's family of believers?

Do you think of yourself as someone who gets along well with others? Why, or why not?

Describe a difficult relationship in which you have been involved.

If you were to consider this relationship in the light of God's grace, how might that change your attitude toward and interaction with him or her?

Embrace the pursuit of healthy relationships through the ministry of the local church.

> *Dear heavenly Father, relating to others offers some of the great challenges of life. I know that I can be prideful, strong-willed, and unwilling to forgive. Allow me to clearly see the life and example of Jesus that I might emulate Him in my relationships within God's family.*

Unity and Compassion

Read 1 Corinthians 12:24–26.

We live in a fragmented world. With so much emphasis on choice and variety, it's only becoming more so. Even new countries seem to be formed every few years. With its thousands of denominations, the church is sadly no stranger to this fragmentation, a point that serves to illustrate the extreme number of issues Christians have found to disagree upon. And with so many options, we have created a culture in which people have almost innumerable choices about where they go to church.

In such a culture, it becomes more difficult than ever to pursue unity—the ideal of the local church that Paul outlined in 1 Corinthians 12:24–26. The Bible teaches that there should be no division among believers, and instead we ought to care for one another. Therefore, the Christian who is committed to the local church embraces a life of unity and compassion. When we have committed to a local body for the long haul, we give ourselves the opportunity to exercise compassion and work through the issues that leave us in danger of division.

Look back at 1 Corinthians 12:25–26. What is the connection Paul makes between division and caring?

What is the connection he makes regarding suffering and rejoicing?

How do these connections illustrate our unity?

When we have committed ourselves to a local body through the unity of our Christian faith, the list of reasons why we might divide becomes significantly shorter. Conflict over finances, politics, musical styles, or even the layout of the worship bulletin can become an opportunity to exhibit grace in the midst of different opinions. In such moments, we learn to see the conflict as an unfortunate circumstance that can be resolved in love. And when Christians work toward unity in the context of God's people—regardless of different musical tastes or political opinions—the light of our faith will shine brighter than ever in a world characterized by fragmentation.

Describe some of the struggles you have had in being unified with other Christians.

How have you contributed to these conflicts or divisions?

Think about a particular conflict that remains unresolved. What steps will you take to resolve it with compassion and grace?

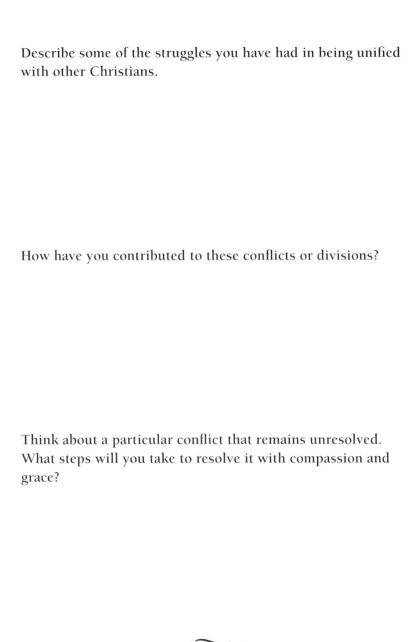

As you think about your local church attendance, seek to make it a time in which you can practice living in unity and compassion with others.

> *Dear Father, Your Son died and rose from the dead so that we might find unity in Him. Yet I see in my own life numerous examples of small and large divisions among Christians. Strengthen me, Lord, that I might be able to be an influence for grace in the midst of conflict.*

The Freedom to Love and Serve

Read Galatians 5:1, 13–14.

One of the primary reasons many Christians leave their churches comes down to one word: *legalism*. When a church embraces legalism, people are browbeaten and then pressed into rigid molds of behavior that usually have little to do with the clear commands of Scripture. Sadly, these churches often have more in common with the Pharisees of the New Testament than they do with Christ.

How far this picture is from what God has created the church to be! As members of the local church, we are meant to live in liberty, love, and service. Paul reminded us in Galatians 5:13 that we are a people called to freedom. However, this is not to be taken as an opportunity to indulge our sinful instincts (Galatians 5:14). It should be embraced as an opportunity to freely exhibit love and to graciously serve hurting and suffering people both inside and outside our congregations. Both believers and nonbelievers receive more than enough bullying and intimidation from the world. God has called us to demonstrate to them something vastly different—His hope and His compassion.

Matthew 9:11–13 describes one of Jesus's interactions with the Pharisees, a group of religious leaders in His day. What were the Pharisees concerned about? Why do you think Jesus's actions bothered them?

What was Jesus's response to the Pharisees' question?

How does Jesus's response inform your understanding of this debate between legalism and freedom in the Christian life?

Often, the tendency toward legalism comes from a good start—it develops out of a desire to live well for Christ. However, when those desires stretch beyond the commands of Scripture and when those rules begin to become markers of "true faith" for us and others, our churches slip into the pit of legalism.

The attractiveness of legalism is based on the apparent righteousness it pursues, but its danger lies in the way it discards grace. Therefore, we must avoid legalism at all costs, or our churches might be in danger of losing the very thing that brought us to Christ in the first place—God's grace.

What does freedom in Christ mean to you?

How would you advise someone to pursue a life lived in grace?

The church belongs to Jesus, who calls us to pursue healthy relationships in a spirit of unity and compassion. This should lead us to live lives of liberty, love, and service with our brothers and sisters in Christ.

> *Gracious Father, lead me into a life of grace and mercy toward others. Remind me of Your Son's sacrifice on my behalf as I seek to serve Your creatures in love. Help me to depend on You as I seek to grow and mature in my commitment to Your church.*

How to Begin a Relationship with God

We all encounter plenty of distractions as we journey along life's road. The modern world provides conveniences and comforts unlike anything that's ever been seen in human history. We can become blinded to our need for spiritual growth. One of the keys to the Christian life is recognizing our need to grow, to be transformed by God into His ideal for our lives. But without a relationship with Him, we cannot grow spiritually.

Spiritual growth in the Christian life depends upon the possession of a solid foundation in Jesus Christ. He is faithful to lovingly guide, direct, and empower us as we draw near to Him. The Bible marks the path to God with four essential truths. Let's look at each marker in detail.

Our Spiritual Condition:
Totally Depraved

The first truth is rather personal. One look in the mirror of Scripture, and our human condition becomes painfully clear:

> There is none righteous, not even one;
> There is none who understands,
> There is none who seeks for God;
> All have turned aside, together they have
>   become useless;
> There is none who does good,
> There is not even one. (Romans 3:10–12)

We are all sinners through and through—totally depraved. Now, that doesn't mean we've committed every atrocity known to humankind. We're not as *bad* as we can be, just as *bad off* as we can be. Sin colors all our thoughts, motives, words, and actions.

You still don't believe it? Look around. Everything around us bears the smudge marks of our sinful nature. In spite of our best efforts to create a perfect world, crime statistics continue to soar, divorce rates keep climbing, and families keep crumbling.

Something has gone terribly wrong in our society and in ourselves—something deadly. Contrary to how the world would repackage it, "me-first" living doesn't equal rugged individuality and freedom; it equals death. As Paul said in his letter to the Romans, "The wages of sin is death" (Romans 6:23)—our spiritual and physical death that comes from God's righteous judgment of our sin, along with all of the emotional and practical effects of this separation that we experience on a daily basis. This brings us to the second marker: God's character.

God's Character: Infinitely Holy

How can God judge each of us for a sinful state we were born into? Our total depravity is only half the answer. The other half is God's infinite holiness.

The fact that we know things are not as they should be points us to a standard of goodness beyond ourselves. Our sense of injustice in life on this side of eternity implies a perfect standard of justice beyond our reality. That standard and source is God Himself. And God's standard of holiness contrasts starkly with our sinful condition.

Scripture says that "God is Light, and in Him there is no darkness at all" (1 John 1:5). God is absolutely holy — which creates a problem for us. If He is so pure, how can we who are so impure relate to Him?

Perhaps we could try being better people, try to tilt the balance in favor of our good deeds, or seek out methods for self-improvement. Throughout history, people have attempted to live up to God's standard by keeping the Ten Commandments or living by their own code of ethics. Unfortunately, no one can come close to satisfying the demands of God's law. Romans 3:20 says, "By the works of the Law no flesh will be justified in His sight; for through the Law comes the knowledge of sin."

Our Need: A Substitute

So here we are, sinners by nature and sinners by choice, trying to pull ourselves up by our own bootstraps to attain a relationship with our holy Creator. But every time we try, we fall flat on our faces. We can't live a good enough life to make up for our sin, because God's standard isn't "good enough"—it's *perfection*. And we can't make amends for the offense our sin has created without dying for it.

Who can get us out of this mess?

If someone could live perfectly, honoring God's law, and would bear sin's death penalty for us—in our place—then we would be saved from our predicament. But is there such a person? Thankfully, yes!

Meet your substitute—*Jesus Christ*. He is the One who took death's place for you!

> [God] made [Jesus Christ] who knew no
> sin to be sin on our behalf, so that we might
> become the righteousness of God in Him.
> (2 Corinthians 5:21)

God's Provision: A Savior

God rescued us by sending His Son, Jesus, to die on the cross for our sins (1 John 4:9–10). Jesus was fully human and fully divine (John 1:1, 18), a truth that ensures His understanding of our weaknesses, His power to forgive, and His ability to bridge the gap between God and us (Romans 5:6–11). In short, we are "justified as a gift by His grace through the redemption which is in Christ Jesus" (3:24). Two words in this verse bear further explanation: *justified* and *redemption*.

Justification is God's act of mercy, in which He declares believing sinners righteous, while they are still in their sinning state. Justification doesn't mean that God *makes* us righteous, so that we never sin again, rather that He *declares* us righteous — much like a judge pardons a guilty criminal. Because Jesus took our sin upon Himself and suffered our judgment on the cross, God forgives our debt and proclaims us PARDONED.

Redemption is Christ's act of paying the price to release us from sin's bondage. God sent His Son to bear His wrath for all of our sins — past, present, and future (Romans 3:24 – 26; 2 Corinthians 5:21). In humble obedience, Christ willingly endured the shame of the cross for your sake (Mark 10:45; Romans 5:6 – 8; Philippians 2:8). Christ's death satisfied God's righteous demands. He no longer holds your sins against you, because His own Son paid the penalty for them. You are freed from the slave market of death, never to be a slave again!

Placing Your Faith in Christ

These four truths describe how God has provided a way to Himself through Jesus Christ. Because the price has been paid in full by God, we must respond to His free gift of eternal life in total faith and confidence in Him to save us. We must step forward into the relationship with God that He has prepared for us — not by doing good works or by being a good person but by coming to Him just as we are and accepting His justification and redemption by faith.

> For by grace you have been saved through faith;
> and that not of yourselves, it is the gift of God;
> not as a result of works, so that no one may
> boast. (Ephesians 2:8–9)

We accept God's gift of salvation simply by placing our faith in Christ alone for the forgiveness of our sins. Would you like to enter a relationship with your Creator by trusting in Christ as your Savior? If so, here's a simple prayer you can use to express your faith:

> *Dear God,*
>
> *I know that my sin has put a barrier between You and me. Thank You for sending Your Son, Jesus, to die in my place. I trust in Jesus alone to forgive my sins, and I accept His gift of eternal life. I ask Jesus to be my personal Savior and the Lord of my life. Thank You. In Jesus's name, amen.*

If you've prayed this prayer or one like it and you wish to find out more about knowing God and His plan for you in the Bible, contact us at Insight for Living. You can speak to one of our pastors on staff by using the information below:

> Insight for Living
> Pastoral Ministries Department
> Post Office Box 269000
> Plano, Texas 75026-9000
> USA
> 972-473-5097 (Monday through Friday,
> 8:00 a.m.–5:00 p.m. Central time)
> www.insight.org/contactapastor

Resources for Probing Further

S piritual growth is more often sought than achieved. And in a world desperate for voices of truth, few pursuits are more significant for those who follow Christ than maturing in our faith. To achieve such growth requires several things: knowledge of the Scriptures so that we know where we are headed; community, which allows others in our lives to help guide our steps and remind us of what's significant in life; and perseverance, which ensures that we make real strides in our spiritual development.

This devotional has been one step along the path of your spiritual growth. To further your study, we recommend the following resources. Of course, we cannot always endorse everything a writer or ministry says, so we encourage you to approach these and all other non-biblical resources with wisdom and discernment.

Bonhoeffer, Dietrich. *The Cost of Discipleship*. New York: Touchstone, 1995.

Bounds, E. M. *Power through Prayer*. Chicago: Moody Publishers, 1985.

Foster, Richard J. *Celebration of Discipline: The Path to Spiritual Growth*. San Francisco: HarperSanFrancisco, 1988.

Hendricks, Howard, and William Hendricks. *Living by the Book: The Art and Science of Reading the Bible*. Chicago: Moody Publishers, 1991.

Kreeft, Peter. *You Can Understand the Bible: A Practical and Illuminating Guide to Each Book in the Bible*. Fort Collins, Colo.: Ignatius Press, 2005.

Stott, John. *Christian Basics: An Invitation to Discipleship*. Grand Rapids: Baker Books, 2003.

Swindoll, Charles R. *Growing Deep in the Christian Life*. Grand Rapids: Zondervan, 1995.

Swindoll, Charles R., and Greg Laurie. *Passion for the Gospel*. Plano, Tex.: IFL Publishing House, 2006.

Swindoll, Charles R. *So, You Want to be Like Christ? Eight Essentials to Get You There*. Nashville: W Publishing, 2005.

Swindoll, Charles R. *The Strength of Character: 7 Essential Traits of a Remarkable Life*. Nashville: J. Countryman, 2007.

Tozer, A. W. *The Pursuit of God: The Human Thirst for the Divine*. Camp Hill, Penn.: WingSpread, 2007.

Walvoord, John F., and Roy B. Zuck, eds. *The Bible Knowledge Commentary: New Testament*. Wheaton, Ill.: Victor Books, 1983.

Walvoord, John F., and Roy B. Zuck, eds. *The Bible Knowledge Commentary: Old Testament*. Wheaton, Ill.: Victor Books, 1985.

Ordering Information

If you would like to order additional copies of *Practical Christian Living: A Road Map to Spiritual Growth* or other Insight for Living resources, please contact the office that serves you.

United States

Insight for Living
Post Office Box 269000
Plano, Texas 75026-9000
USA
1-800-772-8888
Monday through Thursday, 7:00 a.m. – 9:00 p.m., and Friday, 7:00 a.m. – 7:00 p.m. Central time
www.insight.org
www.insightworld.org

Canada

Insight for Living Canada
Post Office Box 2510
Vancouver, BC V6B 3W7
CANADA
1-800-663-7639
www.insightforliving.ca

Australia, New Zealand, and South Pacific

Insight for Living Australia
Post Office Box 1011
Bayswater, VIC 3153
AUSTRALIA
1 300 467 444
www.insight.asn.au

United Kingdom and Europe

Insight for Living United Kingdom
Post Office Box 348
Leatherhead
KT22 2DS
UNITED KINGDOM
0800 915 9364
www.insightforliving.org.uk

Other International Locations

International constituents may contact the U.S. office through our Web site (www.insightworld.org), mail queries, or by calling +1-972-473-5136.

Notes